# DREAMING *of* EAST

D Wilkie Constantinople October 1840

# DREAMING *of* EAST

### WESTERN WOMEN
### *and the* EXOTIC ALLURE
### *of the* ORIENT

## BARBARA HODGSON

GREY**S**TONE BOOKS
Douglas & McIntyre Publishing Group
Vancouver/Toronto/Berkeley

Greystone Books
A division of Douglas & McIntyre Ltd.
2323 Quebec Street, Suite 201
Vancouver, British Columbia
V5T 4S7
www.greystonebooks.com

*Library and Archives Canada Cataloguing in Publication Data*

Hodgson, Barbara, 1955–
    Dreaming of East : western women and the exotic allure of the
Orient / Barbara Hodgson.

Includes bibliographical references and index.
ISBN 13: 978-1-55365-118-5
ISBN 10: 1-55365-118-9

    1. Women travelers—Middle East—History. 2. Women travelers—Europe—
History. 3. Middle East—Description and travel. 4. Women—Middle East—
History—18th century. 5. Women—Middle East—History—19th century. I. Title.

DS48.H62 2005          915.604´15´082          C2005-901194-7

Library of Congress information is available upon request.

FRONTISPIECE: *Mme Josephine, 1840.* Artist Sir David Wilkie was a guest at Mme Josephine's popular hotel in Constantinople. Wilkie, *Sir David Wilkie Sketches,* 1843, pl. 24.
TITLE PAGE: *Female musician.* Edward W. Lane, *The Thousand and One Nights,* vol. 2, 1883, 69.
PAGE VII: *"Tourists ascending the Great Pyramid,"* 1910–20. American Colony photo, courtesy Library of Congress LC-DIG-matpc-01498.

Edited by Nancy Flight
Copyedited by Wendy Fitzgibbons
Design by Barbara Hodgson/Byzantium Books
Printed and bound in China by C&C Offset
Distributed in the U.S. by Publishers Group West

The publisher gratefully acknowledges the assistance of the Canada Council for the Arts and of the British Columbia Ministry of Community, Aboriginal and Women's Services. The publisher also acknowledges the financial support of the Government of Canada through the Book Publishing Industry Development Program (BPIDP) for its publishing activities.

All uncredited images are from Byzantium Archives. Images without attribution are from unknown sources or by unknown artists. Every effort has been made to trace accurate ownership of copyrighted text and visual material used in this book. Errors or omissions will be corrected in subsequent editions, provided notification is sent to the publisher.

# Contents

MEDITERRANEAN
EGYPTIAN
ADRIATIC
CRUISES

STEAMSHIP AGENCY
FIFTH AVENUE
(Moeder Side)
PITTSBURGH, PA.

# CUNARD LINE

*The breath of the desert is liberty.*—Isabel Burton, 1893

# Introduction

## DREAMING OF EAST

ISABEL BURTON venerated three ideals: Richard Burton, the East, and Liberty. During her stay in Damascus between 1869 and 1871, she experienced all three and, for those years, lived what she considered a perfect life. Her exhilaration with this state of affairs spilled over into her book *The Inner Life of Syria,* in which she breathlessly admitted that the slightest reference to her beloved Damascus brought tears to her eyes and made her "heart throb."[1]

Her husband, Richard, an audacious adventurer, was an understandable ideal, but the East *and* liberty? That Isabel Burton connected these two seemingly contradictory concepts, and that she was just one of many Western women to do so, is especially intriguing.

The first such woman to associate the East and liberty may have been Lady Mary Wortley Montagu in 1717. An early traveler to Turkey, she wrote copious letters rhapsodizing about the *Arabian Nights* atmosphere she found there. As her journey was made soon after that book's instantly popular translation into French as *Les Mille et une nuits* (the first time it was available in a European language, quickly followed by an English translation), her effusive reports heightened the romance of those tales and stimulated the growing taste for things Oriental. Captivated by her

*Cunard Line cruises.*
Tourist brochure, 1914.

descriptions of Turkish attire and by portraits of her in these garments, readers hastened to add turbans, pantaloons, and caftans to their wardrobes. Her letters, however, also provoked questions about liberty. By praising the freedoms she believed were enjoyed by Eastern women, and by describing those she herself experienced, Montagu influenced generations of women, who, in their own travels to the East, sought this vaunted liberty for themselves.

Why women should seek freedom in the East has long fascinated me. How could a region where women are secluded and restricted possibly offer others a liberty denied to them in their own, more liberal countries?

*Lady Mary Wortley Montagu, 1720.* Sir Godfrey Kneller, artist. Montagu, *The Works of the Right Honourable Lady Mary Wortley Montagu,* vol. 1, 1803, frontispiece.

To explore this question, I look at women who went to the eastern Ottoman Empire—Egypt, Palestine, Syria, Iraq, and Turkey—from 1717 until 1930, almost ten years after the empire's collapse. Through examples of individuals and their modes of travel, dress, motivations, attitudes, and dealings with the people they met, I let the travelers themselves show how they found freedom and how their experiences were provocative, unsettling, and, ultimately, catalytic.

The interpretation of freedom changes through time and place, and the West underwent several radical shifts during the period covered in this book. From the tolerant years of the Enlightenment, through stretches of social upheaval and revolution, into the constraints and contradictions of Victoria's reign, and up to the momentous changes of the early twentieth century, women had fluctuating but limited rights in matters of divorce, property, children, and wages. They were also, for the most part, discouraged from pursuing independent thought or inquiry.

Travel to the East offered a woman escape from convention and filled gaps in her education. She found, as well, that her meager knowledge seemed prodigious in comparison with that of Eastern women, who had even less formal schooling. This discovery gave her an unaccustomed confidence and incentive to learn more. To those of the East she formed a new category of gender, a being with the learning of a man and the appearance of a woman, to be treated with near equality. All too used to an inferior status at home, women found this venture into the land of near sexlessness stimulating and disturbing. Isabel Burton believed that once smitten by the East a woman was no longer fit for her former life.[2]

Not all women desired the opportunity to break loose, for what one saw as unreasonable repression seemed appropriate to another. Just as some sought a release from their bonds, others saw no need for change. There were also those who, when taken to live in the East by their fathers or husbands, wanted no more than to re-create old ways in new locales.

By displacing themselves, the women in these pages—Burton and Montagu, as well as Princess Cristina di Belgiojoso, Gertrude Bell, and Ida Pfeiffer, to name a few—were able, through comparison and distance, to assess who they were and who they thought they should or could be. They circumvented restrictions through ingenuity or outright defiance and proved that they were capable of managing their own lives. They compared their own relative independence with the sequestered lives of Eastern women, and some even found enviable elements of liberty within the harems, which they considered to be outside the control of men.

Readers contemporaneous with the travelers included here would have understood references and attitudes that may bewilder us now. We are inclined to judge the older accounts in the context of the present day, but we need to make allowances for earlier times. For example, a woman whose appearance or conduct attracted attention also provoked disapproval. Few were willing to renounce society's approbation, so unless they were very rich or very poor they advanced cautiously. Another feature of the age was the cultivation of such feminine graces as excessive timidity. Many women, even those apparently capable of intrepid travel, indulged in absurd displays of weakness. Some were also prone to making seemingly vain and outrageous claims.

Women in the West who desired independence often had difficulty reconciling this desire with their expectation of masculine deference. But when in the East, they reaped the benefits of being treated almost as men—especially regarding freedom of movement and respect for their opinions—while still being accorded the protectiveness customarily due to them as women.

Women from all levels of society traveled to the East. From their disparate personalities I have found it impossible to generalize about their attitudes toward the people and countries they visited. French aristocrats differed from their German, Italian, and English counterparts and from each other. In turn, they all differed from the far-from-harmonious middle class. Working-class women had little in common with those in more advantageous positions.

Of the numerous reasons women gave for heading East, of particular interest here are escape, curiosity, and wanderlust. Since the publication of Edward Said's *Orientalism* in 1978, and the subsequent debates, it is no longer possible to write about European women in the East without some reference to Orientalism, feminism, and imperialism. That said, this book is not about these aspects of Western culture; it is about women who did not fit in.

As I discovered during research for my previous book on women's travel, *No Place for a Lady,* most accounts available to us today are by British women. The culture of travel hit the British Isles earlier than elsewhere in Europe, and publishers quickly capitalized on this exploding interest. Women writers were immensely popular, as their perspective of travel differed from that of men, and, then as now, readers were amazed that a woman could venture intrepidly into the unknown and live to write about it. Aside from the many who wrote books or whose letters and diaries survive, many more left only tantalizing hints, but even some of these glimpses support the idea of independence. There was Countess Talbot, for example, who, according to gossip overheard by a Captain Hanson in Alexandria in 1819, climbed to the top of Pompey's Pillar.[3] For those interested in numbers, I have found references to some 240 British female travelers to the East from 1717 until 1930, compared with 58 from France, 28 from German-speaking countries, and 23 from elsewhere on the Continent, including Italy, Denmark, and Holland. I also found nearly 100 American women, a third of whom published accounts, many of which emphasized pilgrimage. There were relatively few accounts of Canadian, Australian, and New Zealand women traveling.

I have not included accounts given during times of war or other conflict, as these are not true reflections of a country in its normal state. Women such as Zetton Buchanan, held captive during a revolt in Mesopotamia in 1920, and Alice Poulleau, skirting bombs in Damascus in 1925, could be the subjects of a different study.

The pages that follow present a group of very special women who were raised to do anything but travel in distant lands. They should have been wives of peers, writers of gentle novels, painters of flowers, and mothers of happy families. Instead, they hopped aboard boats and made their way to Alexandria, Beirut, Constantinople. They hired guides and horses, slept in tents or rough inns, and did their best to understand new manners and customs. Most important, they lived out their dreams of travel.

---

Note: Arabic and old Turkish spelling variations of almost any single word are seemingly endless. Take, for example, *takhtarawan*, a palanquin. Travelers have called this a *takhtrouan, takkirawan,* and *tarta-a-van.* Except in quotes, where I keep the original spellings, I use transliterations given in Hans Wehr's *Dictionary of Modern Written Arabic.* For place names now altered, I use the original version, such as "Constantinople" rather than "Istanbul." For names with several spellings, I conform to *Merriam-Webster's Geographical Dictionary.* Where *Webster's* is mute, I defer to *The Times Atlas of the World.*

*Few such moments of exhilaration can come as that which stands at the threshold of wild travel. The gates of the enclosed garden are thrown open, . . . with a wary glance to right and left you step forth, and, behold! the immeasurable world.*—Gertrude Bell, 1907

# Setting the Stage

## WESTERN WOMEN & EASTERN TRAVEL

GERTRUDE BELL, writing of her 1905 trek from Jerusalem to Damascus through the seldom-visited Hauran, a plateau region south of Damascus, captures the excitement she felt as she set off. Her enchantment with the East survived her subsequent travels and her nine-year residence in Baghdad.

This book focuses on the area that Bell and others came to know well: the eastern portion of the former Ottoman Empire, specifically, Turkey, Syria, Palestine, Mesopotamia, and Egypt, though at times the boundaries are stretched to include Persia and North Africa. Once known as "the Orient," or "the East," this region is now called "the Middle East," a vague term coined in the early twentieth century. In these pages, the first two labels are used in the context of the eighteenth and nineteenth centuries.

This region was, and still is, home to many ethnic and religious groups. Turkey is now predominantly Muslim, but in the nineteenth century and earlier its population of Turks, Europeans (especially Greek), Armenians, Kurds, Arabs, and Jews practiced variations of Islam, Christianity, and Judaism. Syria now, as in the past, boasts Arabs, Kurds, Armenians, Turks, Jews, and Druze. Egypt can be divided into Copts, Arabs, Nubians (Upper Egyptians), Turks, Armenians, Jews, Levantines, and Europeans.

*Damascus café.* C. Werner, artist; C. Bertrand, engraver. Wilson, *Picturesque Palestine*, 1881, vol. 1, facing p. 408.

*Turkey in Asia.* Philips *Comprehensive Atlas,* 1871.

Everywhere are city dwellers, fellahin (farmers), and Bedouin, or Bedu (nomads).

Choosing the correct way to refer to such a heterogeneous populace is difficult. In the past, "Turk" described inhabitants of Turkey, and "Arab" was used for all people from Syria, Palestine, Iraq, Arabia, and Egypt. As the term "Arab," especially, can be misleading, and as it is too cumbersome to constantly list the various peoples, I use the all-encompassing word "Eastern." Where appropriate, however, nationalities or ethnic groups are specified.

By the same token, "Western" will have to do for the diverse peoples from Europe and North America. Again, where appropriate, "European," "British," "French," and so on are

used. For the purposes of this book, "Western" women, whom I also refer to as "European," are those from outside the Ottoman Empire, excluding women from Greece and other countries of what was known as "Turkey in Europe." A brief look at the area as it was during the periods covered will not be out of place here.

## THE OTTOMAN EMPIRE

At its greatest extent, the Ottoman Empire included North Africa, from Egypt to Morocco; eastern Europe, from Greece to Hungary; and Syria and Mesopotamia (today's Iraq). From 1453, it was ruled by sultans from Constantinople, also called the Sublime Porte. Turkish was the language of government, and Arabic, except in Turkey, the lingua franca. Few travelers to the East would have been insensible of the empire's influence, whether in bureaucracy, law enforcement, or dress.

Trade of silks, cotton, spices, and drugs drew Europeans to the Ottoman Empire. The family of John Barker, English consul to Aleppo from 1799 until 1825, for example, had been traders in the area for generations.

While the European presence and influence in the East increased during the nineteenth century, the Ottoman Empire literally lost ground: Greece was granted independence in 1830, Egypt's viceroy became a hereditary position after 1840, and Tunisia was occupied by France in 1881. Syria, Palestine, and Iraq were lost to the French and British in 1918–20. The sultanate was abolished soon after, and Turkey was declared a republic in 1924.

ABOVE: *Panorama of Palmyra. Chromolithograph from a sketch by Emily Beaufort.* Beaufort, *Egyptian Sepulchres and Syrian Shrines,* 1861, frontispiece.

PREVIOUS PAGE: *Constantinople, "Mosque of Sultana Valide."* W.H. Bartlett, artist. Pardoe, *Beauties of the Bosphorus,* vol. 1, 1839.

## Turkey

For travelers arriving by boat, the first sight of the empire's capital was Stambul's stunning horizon of minarets and domes—a veritable "thousand and one nights," as many wrote. Stambul, now central Istanbul, was one of the city's three main quarters. The other two were Pera, present-day Beyoğlu, the favored base for foreigners across the Golden Horn (the city's harbor), and Scutari, now Üsküdar, where troops were quartered during the Crimean War of 1853–56, situated on the Asian side of the Bosporus, the strait that separates Europe and Asia. Ambassadors had summer residences at Ortaköy, Tarabya, and Belgrade (Lady Montagu's home), villages along the Bosporus and the Golden Horn.

Of all Ottoman cities, Constantinople was the most Europeanized and had received Western women since at least 1717, when Ladies Montagu, Paget, and Winchelsea accompanied their diplomat husbands there for peace negotiations with the Porte. Thereafter, women visited and resided in the city as tourists, entertainers, innkeepers, nurses, governesses, companions, and wives of merchants and diplomats.

Aside from Constantinople, Bursa, to the south, was a

welcome summer retreat; Smyrna, on the coast, was little more than a transit stop. Few women traveled outside these centers, exceptions including Cristina di Belgiojoso, Isabella Bird,* Louisa Jebb, and Gertrude Bell.

### Syria, or the Levant

Syria, including Palestine, was part of the Ottoman Empire from 1516 until 1918, while mountainous Lebanon remained more or less independent. In 1920 and 1923, Syria and Lebanon became French mandates, and Palestine and adjacent Transjordan came under British protection.

Palestine, now known as Israel, or Israel and the West Bank, was long accustomed to foreigners since it was an important destination for pilgrims, who explored its every nook and cranny, from Jerusalem to remote monasteries. In Syria proper, Damascus, vaunted to be the oldest city in the world, preserved its almost mythological status through the difficulties involved in visiting the place. Reputed to be fanatically xenophobic, it forbade consulates until 1832, and the few Westerners there, mostly traders, kept low profiles. Travelers still materialized sporadically,

---

*Bird went by her married name, Bishop, at the time of her Eastern travels, but I refer to her by her more widely known family name here.

*Tourists at Baalbek.*

Lantern slide, c. 1920.

including Hester Stanhope in 1812, oblivious to warnings that she would be attacked. In contrast, Beirut and Tripoli, coastal cities of Lebanon, had accommodated many pilgrims and traders over the centuries. Until the 1860s, it was a major undertaking getting to the archaeological sites of Petra, in what was then known as Arabia, now Jordan; Baalbek, in Lebanon; and especially distant Palmyra, in Syria. Stanhope went to Palmyra in 1813; the next Western woman on record as doing so was Jane Digby, forty years later.

*Egypt*

Egypt, specifically the Nile, became the main destination of nearly all nineteenth-century visitors to the Orient. Europe's reintroduction to this country came from earlier travelers such as James Bruce and the Comte de Volney, from the commotion produced by Napoleon's 1798 invasion, and from antiquities shipped to Europe by Giovanni Belzoni, Baron von Minutoli,★ English consul Henry Salt, and French consul Bernardino Drovetti, all in Egypt from 1800 until the 1820s.

Egypt was a contentious part of the Ottoman Empire, and its connection became even more fragile after 1798. Napoleon's defeat by the British and the Ottomans was followed by the semiautonomous rule of Albanian Muhammad 'Ali Pasha. He and his successors forged strong ties with Europe. In 1882, Egypt was occupied by the British and became a protectorate of that country until 1914. It achieved a quasi independence in 1922.

Western women in Egypt before the nineteenth century were either passing through on their way to India, or living there with their merchant husbands or fathers, or, after 1798, as military

★Belzoni was accompanied by his wife, Sarah, and Minutoli by his wife, Wolfardine. Both women appended accounts of their own experiences in Egypt to their husband's books.

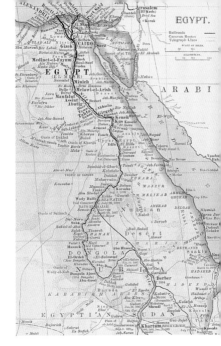

wives. Women's travel to Egypt for travel's sake did not begin until the second decade of the nineteenth century, commencing with the visit of Hester Stanhope. By the 1830s, European women, both travelers and residents, were found mostly in Alexandria or Cairo or in their temporary floating homes on the Nile. Not until 1862, with the arrival of Lucie Duff Gordon at Luxor, do we hear much of their settling south of Cairo.

## Mesopotamia

Mesopotamia, now Iraq, was part of the Ottoman Empire from 1530 until 1920. Its main cities and

*Egypt, c. 1899. The M.-N. Co.*

sites—Baghdad, Babylon, Nineveh, An Najaf, and Mosul—though worthwhile to visit, weren't on a route to anywhere, and travel there was very difficult. Because of Baghdad's proximity to India, the East India Company established a residency there in 1783; a memorable resident was Babylon archaeologist Claudius James Rich, in charge from 1808 until his death in 1821, who was accompanied by his wife, Mary, on his many travels through the country.[1]

In 1848, Ida Pfeiffer was one of the first European women to independently travel through Mesopotamia. After her came Jane Digby, in 1854, followed by Anne Blunt in 1878 and 1879. By the 1900s, however, Western women were well-established visitors and residents, the most famous being Gertrude Bell.

For all its diversity, the eastern Ottoman Empire was a relatively cohesive area to travel around, especially in matters of transport and accommodation. But most travelers arrived with lofty expectations that had little to do with these mundane details. Their imaginations had already provided them with a crystal-clear vision of what they would find.

THE WHITE STAR LINES ★ CRUISE OF THE ARABIC
TO THE MEDITERRANEAN AND THE ORIENT

MADEIRA
SPAIN
MEDITERRANEAN
PALESTINE
& EGYPT.
A TOUR OF
73 DAYS

COSTING ONLY
$400 & UP
INCLUDING
SHORE EXCURSIONS
DRIVES, GUIDES,
HOTELS ⁂ AND
ALL NECESSARY
EXPENSES.

SPHINX & PYRAMIDS

MOSQUE OF OMAR
Jerusalem

## THE ALLURE OF THE EAST

*With each fresh experience, the sense of a glad freedom is interwoven.*
*The traveller knows that joy in living, a joy which our civilisation has*
*done its best to improve away.*—Ella Sykes, 1901[2]

Eastern voyages have often been described as flights from the
enervating effects of progress. For a woman living in the bleak-
ness of northern Europe's Industrial Revolution, especially,
there was much to flee. If she couldn't get away from her never-
changing vista of cold, gray skies, she could always find
temporary escape in the pages of explorers' accounts. By following the exploits of Eastern travelers such as James Bruce,
Jean-Louis Burckhardt, or Carsten Niebuhr, she could experience, for a few hours at least, vicarious thrills and the beckoning
expanses of horizons illuminated by a sun that always seemed
to shine.

At first, women could but dream of this kind of travel; it was
not only alien to them but morally unacceptable and, so they
were repeatedly told, beyond their physical and mental stamina.
But many, by journeying on the Continent, proved to themselves that they were capable travelers. And when they heard
reports of women who ventured farther afield, it seemed possible for them, too.

The average woman still needed meaningful reasons for
travel, as escape or wanderlust only drew criticism. To excuse
her whim, she might claim that her health forced a change of
climate or that she had to follow her husband or chaperone a
young lady. She could point out that a pilgrimage to the Holy
Land was a duty, profess a desire to help her Eastern sisters, or
express a wish to learn.

Orientalism, the study of the cultural aspects of
the East, became a growing influence in the West,
affecting not only scholars but artists and writers
as well. As women encountered the ravishing
paintings of far-off deserts and exotic cities by

*The exotic image of the*
*East was emphasized in*
*this tourist brochure, "The*
*White Star Lines Cruise*
*of the Arabic," 1910.*

Orientalist artists such as Jean-Léon Gérôme, Leopold Carl Müller, and John Frederick Lewis and read fabulous tales of harems, flying carpets, and minarets in the *Arabian Nights* and other Oriental tales, their visions of travel to the East coalesced.

Examples of other travelers, men and women, gave them confidence; guidebooks prepared them for all contingencies; and, most important, paintings and tales fired their imaginations.

## ESCAPE TO THE ARABIAN NIGHTS

*From the world that is, I want to go to that which was. From the West of today to the Orient of yesterday.*—Countess Ida von Hahn-Hahn, 1844[3]

To Westerners, the East was a living museum filled with people, objects, and traditions, recalling a heroic and idealized past. The few shreds of these noble bygone days left in Europe had been trampled upon by countless tourists. Greece held on to a vestige of classical luster, and Spain was considered to be almost North Africa, but by the 1830s they too were dismissed as spoiled. The East, so close geographically, seemed enthrallingly distant in time.

A strong influence on the idea of the East as a magic door to the past was the *Arabian Nights* and its many imitations. These tales had a powerful effect on literature and motivated travel to the East, in part because of Lady Mary Wortley Montagu's testimonies to their veracity. "This, you will say, is but too like the Arabian tales," Montagu declared in 1717, recalling a sumptuous dinner party. "You forget," she continued, somewhat inaccurately, "those very tales were written by an author of this country, and (excepting the enchantments) are a real representation of the manners here."[4]

*"Lalla Rookh," an Oriental epic poem by Thomas Moore.*
Moore, *Lalla Rookh*, 1880 [1817], facing p. 3.

More than a century later, Montagu's words were echoed by Julia Pardoe, who wrote in her *Beauties of the Bosphorus* that she hoped her impending trip to Constantinople would lead to "adventures as numerous and as romantic as those of the 'Thousand and One Nights.'"[5]

Lucie Duff Gordon, who lived in Egypt for nearly six years, never shook the sensation that she had entered the dreamlike world of Harun ar-Rashid. Of going up the Nile in her *dhahabiya,* she wrote, "You can't think what an odd effect it is to take up an English book and read it and then look up and hear the men cry, 'Yah Mohammed' . . . It is the reverse of all one's former life

when one sat in England and read of the East . . . and [I] don't
know whether 'I be I as I suppose I be' or not."[6]

Amelia Edwards described a veiled woman in Cairo, "on the
terraced roof in the midst of a cloud of pigeons. Nothing could
be more simple than the scene . . . nothing, at the same time,
more Eastern, strange, and unreal." Of her travels to Persia (now
Iran) with her brother, Major Percy Sykes, in 1895–96, Ella Sykes
recalled how "the glamour of the East penetrated me from the
first moment of landing on its enchanted shores." Olympe
Audouard drew upon the *Arabian Nights* to portray Cairo as seen
by moonlight from the heights of the Citadel. Travelers roman-
ticizing their impressions of the East are legion.[7]

Isabel Burton cherished similarly romantic images, having
devoured Benjamin Disraeli's Eastern romance, *Tancred,* when
she was young. *Tancred,* she wrote "inspired me with all the
ideas, and the yearning for a wild Oriental life." When Richard
was sent to Damascus as consul, she was ecstatic, for Damascus,
she declared, had been "the dream of my childhood and girl-
hood. I am to live amongst Bedawin Arab chiefs; I shall smell
the desert air; I shall have tents, horses, weapons, and be free, like
Lady Hester Stanhope."[8]

Burton believed Englishwoman Jane Digby emulated
Stanhope by traveling to the East and becoming "more Eastern
than the Easterns." Stanhope, with her turban, robe, and loose
trousers, along with her unorthodox behavior, was, like the
*Arabian Nights,* a metaphor for exotic travel.[9]

Where nostalgic male travelers to the East evoked classical,
pharaonic, or medieval comparisons, women recalled the Bible.
This was understandable for pilgrims to the Holy Land, but
other countries also stimulated religious reverie. Of a visit to
the house of a Copt in a village along the Nile, Lucie Duff
Gordon declared that she had been "acting a passage of the Old
Testament."[10]

A measure of disappointment was in store for these dream-
ers, as the East, though fascinating, was not the repository of
elevated ideals, fantasy, and living history that they sought.

Julia Pardoe, who stayed for six months in Constantinople, admitted that in the face of reality, "much of the mist of romance, indeed, rolled away." She knew what her readers wanted, however, and extolled the city's magical wonders.[11]

Amelia Edwards qualified her idealism:

> It is all so picturesque, indeed, so biblical, so poetical, that one is almost in danger of forgetting that the places are something more than beautiful backgrounds, and that the people are not merely appropriate figures placed there for the delight of sketchers, but are made of living flesh and blood, moved by hopes, and fears, and sorrows, like our own.[12]

*Julia Pardoe.* H. Room, artist; Thomson, engraver. Pardoe, *Beauties of the Bosphorus,* vol. 4, 1839, frontispiece.

No matter how disillusioned they became, many still surrendered to their imaginations. Ella Sykes acknowledged that "although many a time I encountered hard facts, quite sufficient to destroy the romantic illusions of most folk, yet they struck against mine powerlessly."[13]

From Montagu on, women wrote of their anticipation of finding the real *Arabian Nights*. She, Duff Gordon, and Sykes believed they had; Pardoe intimated that this illusion would fade. For most, however, the fanciful images were only part of the allure of the East. No matter how much reality deflated their Oriental dream, they always had the promise of escape and freedom.

## La Femme Libre

*Even in 1927 there is much feeling, chiefly masculine, against a woman venturing into those spheres which, for centuries, have been marked "Strictly preserved. All feminine trespassers will be prosecuted."*—Rosita Forbes, 1928[14]

Rosita Forbes, author of many travel accounts, including *The Secret of the Sahara*, 1921, about her expedition to Al-Kufrah oasis in Libya, had not only trespassed onto the male preserve of exploration but had chosen one of the most jealously guarded regions on earth to do so.

Travelers have a long record of vigorously fending off interlopers of either sex. In 1862, Englishman Samuel Baker raged that Dutch travelers Alexine and Harriet Tinne were turning the remote reaches of the Nile into a tourist playground. Two years later, Richard Burton challenged John Hanning Speke's claim to have found the source of the Nile. In 1905, Mark Sykes was incensed that Gertrude Bell was eyeing his route across Syria. Wilfrid Thesiger belittled Bertram Thomas for having been "bundled" across the Empty Quarter of the Arabian desert by the Bedouin. Freya Stark ignored German explorer Hans Helfritz for accomplishing what she had failed to do in Arabia.[15]

The criticisms men aimed at women who dared step across the line were the same as those they leveled at other men: they were unqualified, they wasted resources, they misbehaved. But whereas men had to prove their incompetence, women were assumed to be unfit. The mere presence of women in Lord Belmore's party at Thebes in 1818 robbed Count Forbin of his desire "to ascend the Nile." He fled, "finding it quite impossible to support the perpetual appearance among the venerable ruins of an English lady's maid in a pink camisole." His outrage, however, did not prevent him from first spending a day with the offending females on

*"La Femme libre," c. 1840. The lady pictured tromps on a law that declares "the wife must obey her husband."*

Allemagne, *Les Saint-Simoniens,* 1930, facing p. 212.

EMANCIPATION

SAPEURS. **Vu ses nombreux services cette troupe tiendra la tête...**

*"Emancipation de la femme: Sapeurs," c. 1840. One of a series of four panels showing how silly it is to expect women to be soldiers. In this case, the man has been obliged to wear a dress.* Allemagne, Prosper Enfantin, 1935, pl. 3.

Belmore's luxurious boat. Forbin's attitude—that women should stay home where they belong—was common.[16]

Turkish and Egyptian dignitaries, on the other hand, treated Englishwoman Sophia Poole with such respect that she wrote, "I am entertained by the most distinguished, not only as an equal, but, generally, as a superior." Poole lived in Cairo in the early 1840s with her brother, Orientalist Edward W. Lane. By pointing out her elevated status in this company, she raised the controversial and key question of equality, giving us a chance to consider how the legal status of nineteenth-century women may have affected their attitudes and their freedom to travel.[17]

There seems to be no evidence that there were special regulations in place to restrict women's travel, whether in mode of transport or in crossing borders. Where passports were necessary, females traveling with male relatives were appended to the man's passport. When unaccompanied, they were given their own documents.

Laws regarding women in Europe and North America pertained mostly to marriage, divorce, and property and had the greatest impact on the middle class. Until 1882, for example, British women ceded their assets to their husbands. In France, after 1881, a woman was allowed to make deposits into bank accounts; it would be a while still before she could withdraw that money. British men could divorce and remarry if their wives were proven adulteresses; women in reciprocal situations could not. Divorce in France—which had been allowed in

1803—was abolished in 1816 and not reinstated until 1884. Regarding property and divorce, as a general rule, of all Western countries the United States was the most advanced. Britain was the most progressive in Europe, and Australia and Canada followed its lead.[18]

Despite, or perhaps because of, the divorce issue, feminism was a vital movement in France until a midcentury backlash halted progress. At the same time, misogynist authors vented their spite toward women writers, referred to as *bas-bleus,* or bluestockings, some of whom retreated behind masculine pseudonyms. In Britain, where the critic's weapon was condescension or satire rather than vitriol, women authors fared better, though a few resorted to pseudonyms or anonymity in hopes that their work would be judged on the basis of merit and not sex.

Not considered to be capable of the same level of rational thought as men, women were discouraged from pursuing political, professional, or scholarly vocations. Because many viewed work as less than respectable, and because a gauge of a family's wealth was the leisure time of its female members, this issue was often irrelevant. In Britain, by roughly 1880 they could study at university but were denied degrees, and they could be nurses but not doctors. Nursing was looked down upon; Florence Nightingale, by salvaging Britain's appalling treatment of its soldiers in the Crimea, turned nursing into an acceptable profession for those who didn't need the money. Teaching and missionary work—also disapproved of—were the only occupations, aside from going into business, becoming a servant, or falling into prostitution, that gave women a chance to travel. It's no surprise that so many took up travel writing to supplement their incomes and justify their wanderings.

The middle-class woman was more likely to consider a career than those born below or above her. If she had an inheritance, her only means of keeping control of it was to remain unmarried and thus be condemned to the pitiable state of spinsterhood. Both author Harriet Martineau, a spinster, and midwife Suzanne Voilquin, separated from her husband, worked to support themselves.

In the nineteenth century, literacy was widespread in northern Europe, and many women learned a second and third language as well. Schooling in the humanities and sciences was at the whim of circumstance and the student's motivation, and some pursued ambitious programs of self-education.

Female suffrage was a secondary issue or even a nonissue for certain women who were otherwise very progressive. Among the more outspoken and intrepid travelers emerged the paradox of the antifeminist feminist: women who saw no need to change legal status, as they never met an obstacle they could not overcome. Believing that success came through an individual's efforts, many rejected the idea of women's rights at some point in their lives. Lady Annie Brassey thought the vote would deprive women of their already considerable power. Gertrude Bell was a founding member of the Anti-Suffrage League in 1908. However, she would have voted in Britain's 1918 elections if she had been home, and by 1921 she was supporting the emancipation of women of the East.[19]

Women in the nineteenth century were very much divided on the issue of female emancipation. Many, content with their situations, felt that their lives would not be improved by getting the vote or having increased responsibilities. The women in this book held varying opinions on this subject but, with a few exceptions, such as the group that follows, were not strong advocates of feminism.

## SAINT-SIMONIENNES

*Woman is the equal of man, will be the equal of man, today she is a
slave, it's her master who must free her.*
—Saint-Simonien creed[20]

In 1834, a small group of lower- and middle-class *femmes eman-
cipées* sailed from Marseilles to Alexandria, their mission to
proselytize and improve the lot of their Egyptian
sisters. They belonged to the Saint-Simoniens, a
movement formed by Count Claude-Henri de
Rouvroy Saint-Simon, which espoused socialist
and utopian views, including female equality. After

*"Saint-Simonienne,
costume théatrical," 1832.*

Allemagne, *Les Saint-Simoniens,* 1930,
facing p. 274.

Saint-Simon's death in 1825, his philosophy was carried on by
Barthèlmy Prosper Enfantin, known as Père Enfantin.

In 1833, Enfantin led his male followers, a learned crowd of
engineers, doctors, and musicians, to Egypt where, it was
prophesied, he would find the "Mère," the Female Messiah, a
vital step for uniting the world. Their motto was *Ce n'est plus
un voyage en Orient, c'est un voyage vers la Femme.* These long-
haired, bearded men would have made a startling sight on the
docks of Alexandria, dressed in their scarlet berets and vests,
belted black tunics, white scarves, and tight red trousers.[21]

They planned to build a canal at Suez, a symbolic and practical means of uniting East and West. But Egypt's ruler,
Muhammad 'Ali, showed no interest in their proposal, so they
turned to other projects—building a dam in the Nile Delta and
establishing an engineering school—and gradually forgot their
mission to find the Mère.★

In the meantime, Enfantin urged Saint-Simoniennes to join
them. At least ten, including Suzanne Voilquin, responded.
Born into poverty, Voilquin had worked at a series of low-
paying jobs and married the syphilitic M. Voilquin. A fervent
supporter of female emancipation, she joined the Saint-
Simoniens in 1832, then she and her husband separated, and she
began writing articles for the periodical *La Femme libre.* Her
arrival in Egypt in December 1834 coincided with an outbreak
of plague that was to kill some 35,000 people in Cairo alone,
including a number of Saint-Simoniens.

She took a room in Old Cairo, first doing laundry, then nursing plague victims at a hospital run by French doctor Clot Bey.
After the plague subsided, Voilquin turned to midwifery. Her
nursing was interrupted by her own illness, then by her pregnancy by an unidentified man. Her child lived only a few weeks.

In September 1836, she returned to Paris, where she tried
but failed to establish a home for pregnant girls. In 1838,

---

★The canal became a reality in 1869, instigated by Ferdinand de Lesseps, who had
  been the French vice-consul at Alexandria in the 1830s.

frustrated with France, she went to Russia and stayed there for eight years. From 1849 to about 1860, she lived in the United States. Her book *Souvenirs d'une fille du peuple,* published posthumously in 1865, chronicled her Egyptian experience.

Another Saint-Simonienne, Clorinde Rogé, whose husband had gone to Algiers for Enfantin, went to Egypt to establish a girls school. To that end, she got the ear of Soliman Pasha al-Faransawi, the former Colonel Joseph Sève of Napoleon's Egyptian army and now a Muslim and high-ranking official in Muhammad 'Ali's court. Rogé, said to be the prettiest of the Saint-Simoniennes, lived for a time in Soliman Pasha's Cairo palace overlooking the Nile, though it is not known if they were lovers. With his help, she visited even the most closed of harems and began proselytizing in earnest but in vain; language differences created insurmountable barriers. She was reunited with her husband in 1836; a short time later the couple went to Constantinople via Lebanon, where they tried to no avail to visit Hester Stanhope.[22]

*Muhammad 'Ali Pasha, viceroy of Egypt, followed by Soliman Pasha al-Faransawi (Colonel Sève).*
Ivray, *L'Aventure Saint-Simonienne et les femmes,* 1928, facing p. 192.

Of Mlle Agarithe Caussidère less is known. She has been called an ex-prostitute, but she was also described as an active participant in the Lyon Insurrection of 1834, distributing cartridges to the workers. When her father and brother were killed during the revolt, she found it expedient to make herself scarce. After wangling a passport in another name, she left for Egypt.[23]

Saint-Simoniennes went to Egypt with the hope of gaining, through their utopian philosophy and actions, the independence that was so elusive in France. Their idealism was misplaced. Egyptians tolerated them but did not adopt their doctrines; plague and poverty reduced their objectives to mere survival. Male Saint-Simoniens, in spite of their averred desire for equality among the sexes, took emancipation only so far.

## IN EXILE
### Princess Cristina di Belgiojoso (1808–71)

*I noted many European-style edifices [in Syria] that reminded me of certain hôtels-de-ville in Normandy. That their aspect is sombre is sad in itself, but there is no sadness in them for the exile, for they remind her of her distant country.*—Cristina di Belgiojoso, 1855[24]

Italian aristocrat Princess Cristina di Belgiojoso traveled independently through Turkey to the Holy Land in 1852. She wished to learn something of the region and to make a pilgrimage, but that she was there at all was the result of exile from Austrian-ruled Lombardy. Known as an agitator and spied upon by the secret police, Belgiojoso fled when police searched her home and found her dead secretary, Gaetano Stelzi, embalmed and neatly dressed, stuffed in a closet. She went first to Athens, then to Turkey, where she bought a small farm in the valley of Eiaq-Maq-Oglou (meaning, roughly, the Son of the Gunflint), on the shores of the Bosporus, two days by horse from Ankara. Osman

*Cristina di Belgiojoso.*
Vincent Vidal, artist. Barbiera, *Passioni del risorgimento*, 1903, frontispiece.

Pasha, its previous owner, sold it to her for the exorbitant sum of 5,000 francs.

In January 1852, she left for an eleven-month journey on horseback to Syria and Palestine, accompanied by her illegitimate daughter, Maria; her English maid, Mrs Parker; and one of Osman's sons. On her way she visited harems, administered medicines, reflected on the customs of the country, and discussed the world with remotely placed muftis. The hardships of winter travel was a recurring topic, as rooms were thick with the fumes of carbon fires, the bitter cold hampered riding, and snow obscured the trails. She constantly questioned the living conditions of the women, whether Turkish, Armenian, or Syrian.

Her route through Syria took her to Latakia and Beirut, then to Sidon, where she stayed at the French khan that was Hester Stanhope's lodging thirty years earlier. After participating in Holy Week ceremonies in Jerusalem, she visited nearby biblical sites.

The farm, to which she returned in December, needed expensive repairs she could not make, as her assets in Italy had been confiscated. To make matters worse, she was attacked and stabbed by one of her employees, a Lombard who had been having an affair with Mrs Parker. Belgiojoso never recovered her health, and she lost the will to stay on.

A strong-willed and independent-minded woman, Belgiojoso traveled with a confidence that is evident in her articles for the periodical *La Revue des deux mondes* and in her book *Asie Mineure et Syrie, souvenirs de voyages.* Unwilling to pander to the ideal of the East, she concluded that "the Syria that I visited . . . scarcely resembles the Syria that I've seen in the books." Her trip raised eyebrows in Paris, where she had also lived in exile. Louise Colet, in her novel *Lui*, referred to her as Princess X, who "went off to Asia to amuse herself with Arabs."[25]

*Sometimes we had nothing to eat through not having arranged for food; and sometimes we slept out in the wet. But does this never happen to those who have made elaborate plans against all possible contingencies?*—Louisa Jebb, 1908

# Little Things Feel the Cold

## THE LOGISTICS OF TRAVEL

LOUISA JEBB, from a "remote agricultural district in the West of England," was the perfect Eastern traveler. She couldn't have cared less about discomforts, and she was, as her companion, "X," wisely realized, qualified to deal "with the male attendants who were incident to our proposed form of travel." X was a student of "comparative religion," with little practical sense.[1]

Not only did X initiate the trip to Turkey and Mesopotamia, she arranged that they begin in winter. When asked why they chose to travel during such an inhospitable season and "along the caravan route which had been long deserted owing to the raids of the Hamidieh Kurds," Jebb responded that she had asked herself that "but had not yet thought of an answer."[2]

Except for Hassan, their Albanian dragoman (from *turjuman,* meaning interpreter) who was with them for nearly seven months, their cooks, escorts, porters, and guides were an ever-changing crew drawn from many ethnic groups. With her sometimes rapacious Armenian cook, Arten, Jebb demonstrated her talent for "dealing with male attendants." She would tell him off in English, which he did not understand:

This method had the advantage of relieving my feelings without hurting his. But there were secret bonds of sympathy between us. We both suffered

*A khan in Smyrna.* James Robertson, artist. *Illustrated London News,* 3 February 1855, 113.

*X on the road.* Jebb, *By Desert Ways to Baghdad*, 1908, facing p. 291.

intensely from the cold, and Arten would carefully wrap things round me so that the apertures and crevices were not on the windward side. There is a good deal of art in this, and he did it very scientifically.

"Little things feel the cold," he would say compassionately, and in such a kindly spirit that, for the moment, I forgave him his greed and forgot to feel undignified.[3]

## GETTING AROUND

*You want to get from one point to another; your wish is passed on, and a mule or an araba appears at your door; and whether it be punctual, or whether, as is more usual in the East, it be late, it is of no consequence, for Time is waiting for you and will wait for ever.*
—Louisa Jebb, 1908[4]

Louisa Jebb's simple observation on the inconsequence of time in the East has been echoed by many travelers. Unhampered by train schedules, hotel reservations, and—unless heading to Jerusalem for Holy Week—firm itineraries, they could take a slow pace in stride and surrender to the anticipation of each new day's venture into the unknown.

In the nineteenth and early twentieth century, the majority of women who traveled to the East were able horsewomen.

This skill, usually cultivated as a pastime, was put to good use for long journeys, since the main method of locomotion in the East was by quadruped. It also gave the women confidence and endurance and brought them a great deal of respect from their guides and porters. Most preferred to ride sidesaddle to accommodate long skirts and to avoid what was bizarrely considered an indecent pose. That underpants were not generally worn until the 1850s was a significant deterrent to riding astride. Sidesaddles were not commonly available in the East, so those determined to ride in this manner were advised to bring their own, as did Anne Blunt for her journey into the Nejd desert.[5]

*Persian* kajaweh. Marcel Dieulafoy, artist; Adrien Marie, engraver. Dieulafoy, *Tour du monde* 48: 1884, 139.

For riding astride, Jebb and X wore divided riding skirts. When Hassan helped them onto their mounts, he would say, "pull it up," then, as he rearranged their skirts for them, he'd say, "pull it down." These two phrases constituted the better part of his stock of English.[6]

Those who preferred not to ride were carried in a variety of litters devised to transport women of the harem, including the *shuqdhuf, kajaweh,* and *takhtarawan.* These contrivances, though cumbersome, allowed women the freedom to travel when horse or mule was not feasible. The traveler could be concealed and thus transported through areas where women might not otherwise have been welcome. And for the traveler who was ill or fatigued, they gave some respite from the demands of riding.

The Arab *shuqdhuf* and Persian *kajaweh,* both constructed of two bedlike platforms that were slung over each side of a camel or mule, were transformed into mobile tents by carpet-

Araba *in Damascus.*

Addison, *Damascus and Palmyra,* 1838,

facing p. 199.

covered lattice frames. According to Rosita Forbes, who had seen a *shuqdhuf* in action, collapse was inevitable "unless both travelers are equal in weight, and unless they both get in and out at exactly the same moment."[7]

The *takhtarawan* of Syria and Turkey was a palanquin carried by mules. Lady Mary Elgin forsook her horse for a stretch and tried one. To climb into it, she had to stand on the back of a man, who knelt down to function as the "The Step." The idea of being crammed into one of these contraptions incensed Hester Stanhope, when her lover, Michael Bruce, and the Aleppo consul, Mr Barker, decided that it would be her transport to Palmyra. "They are coming with a wire thing, a tartavan," Stanhope wrote. "What an absurd idea, in case of danger, to be stuck upon a machine, the tartavangees running away and leaving you to the mercy of two obstinate mules!" She naturally refused it and rode there on horseback.[8]

In contrast, the *araba* and the similarly awkward *telega* humbled their passengers. Lady Elizabeth Craven described these as "vile machine[s] like a covered cart, with rows of benches in the inside. There are no springs to them; and one day . . . I got into one, but chose rather to get out and walk six miles, than be jolted unmercifully."★[9]

Although all modes of transport enabled the traveler to move about more or less freely, Jane Dieulafoy declared that

★Tellingly, words related to *telega,* such as *taluqa, talakhlakha,* and *takhalkhala,* mean, among other things, to dash along, burst forth; shaking, unsteady; to be shaken, and to become disjointed.

riding was the best. The long hours in the saddle were compensated for by being able to "always breathe pure air."[10]

Dhahabiyat *at Bulak.*
Wilhelm Gentz, artist. Ebers, *L'Égypte,* vol. 2, 1883, 164.

In Egypt, the best way to traverse the country was by boat, of which there were at least a dozen types. Travelers ascending the Nile usually hired a *dhahabiya,* the most suitable, as it had cabins. Amelia Edwards, in Egypt during the winter of 1873–74, vividly explained the process of selecting one, which she compared with house hunting:

[The boats] are all built on the same plan, which is not the case with houses; and except as they run bigger or smaller, cleaner or dirtier, are as like each other as twin oysters ... Each Reïs, or captain, displays the certificates given to him by former travelers; and these certificates, being apparently in active circulation, have a mysterious way of turning up again and again on board different boats and in the hands of different claimants. Nor is this all. Dahabeeyahs are given to changing their places, which houses do not do; so that the boat which lay yesterday alongside the eastern bank may be over at the western bank to-day.[11]

Dhahabiya *on the Nile,*
*1860–90.* Photo courtesy Library
of Congress LC-USZ62-104865.

Edwards researched for several hours a day for ten days, trying to keep straight all the different names, features, and captains, before finally securing the *Philae,* a large boat that cost £10 a day, everything included, except wine. Joining her were her companion, "L" (Lucy Renshaw), L's maid (Jennie Lane), "the Happy Couple" (the honeymooning Eyres), their maid (Miss Urquhart), and "the Painter" (Andrew McCallum). The crew of nineteen included head cook Hassan Bedawee and his assistant, dragoman Elias Talhamy, Reïs Hassan, waiters Michael and Habîb, the crew's cook, and twelve sailors.[12]

The distance from Cairo to Wadi Halfa was 964¼ miles. The *Philae* made the round trip in some four months, taking nearly twice the time most took, in order to fulfill Edwards's desire to see every single temple within range.

Edwards remarked on the number of steamers going up and down the Nile. These large, fast boats, some holding as many as one hundred passengers, had first appeared on the Nile in the early 1860s and spelled the demise of leisurely travel by sail. So too did the railway, starting in 1855, when Alexandria and Cairo were connected. The woman who traveled by steamer and rail would have been limited by schedules and immersed in the society of European travelers, and thus deprived of the interactions with Egyptians and the independence experienced by Edwards in the *Philae.*

## WE SLEEP WHERE?

*I've slept on anything or nothing.*—Rosita Forbes, 1928[13]

Today, when travelers to the East think of hotels in Egypt and Turkey, Shepheard's in Cairo and the Pera Palace in Istanbul come to mind. Before these European-style hotels were established, however, there was very little choice of where to stay. A Syrian, Turk, or Egyptian could lodge in a khan, also referred to as a caravanserai or *funduq,* a large building with a central courtyard created for merchants and their animals and wares. Latrines were primitive, and there was no separation of the sexes unless the traveler paid for a separate room—if one was even available.

*"Mrs. Bishop's [Isabella Bird's] tent on her ride amongst the Bakhtiari Lurs." Bird stands on the right. Stoddart, The Life of Isabella Bird, 1906, facing p. 228.*

Isabella Bird pitched her tent in the courtyard of a khan in Iraq, only to find sheep tripping over the guy wires. In another khan, in Persia, the temperature inside dipped to minus 16°F, and snow had to be shoveled out of her room.[14]

Bird described her grim lodgings in the Iraqi town of Ba'qubah:

There is a large square yard, heaped with dirt and rubbish, round which are stables and some dark, ruinous rooms. A broken stair leads to a flat mud roof, on which are some narrow "stalls,"—*rooms* they cannot be called,—with rude doors fastening only from the outside, for windows small round holes mostly stuffed with straw near the roof, for floors sodden earth, for fireplaces holes in the same, the walls slimy and unplastered, the corners full of ages of dusty cobwebs, both the walls and the rafters of the roof black with ages of smoke, and beetles and other abominations hurry into crannies, when the doors are opened, to emerge as soon as they are shut. A small hole in the wall outside each stall serves for cooking. The habits of the people are repulsive, foul odours are only hibernating, and so, mercifully, are the vermin.[15]

Gertrude Bell camped where possible, but in Beydaği, Turkey, in 1907, she slept in a corner of a khan, separated from muleteers and camel drivers by a rough plank wall. Set up with her cot, she was pleased with her niche, but Fattuh, her dragoman, thought it beneath her.[16]

At the other end of the spectrum was a Crusader castle. When Bell approached Qal'at al Hisn, the Krac des Chevaliers, in Syria, little did she know she would be sleeping inside it that night. She rode her horse through the high portal

into a vaulted corridor which covered a broad winding stair. It was almost pitch dark, lighted only by a few loop-holes . . . we turned corner after corner and passed under gateway after gateway until at length we came into the court in the centre of the keep. I felt as if I were somebody in the Faery Queen, and almost expected to see written upon the last arch, "Be not too bold."[17]

In the early nineteenth century, travelers could stay with consuls, but convents, also called monasteries, were another possibility. St Catherine's at Mount Sinai lodged anyone carrying a letter of introduction from its affiliated convent in Cairo. Once bona fides were established, the visitor was lifted up to

the door high above the ground by means of a windlass. *Murray's* guidebook advised women "who may not relish this aërial voyage" to enter the garden by a small gate and from there follow a "dark subterraneous passage to within the convent walls."[18]

*The Convent of Mar Saba.* W. H. Bartlett, artist. Stebbing, *The Christian in Palestine,* [1847], facing p. 183.

Although convents abounded in Syria and Palestine, few were open to women. To stay at Mar Saba, for example, a man needed only to show a letter from the Greek patriarch, but under no circumstances could a woman gain admittance. The number of women turned away from Mar Saba is interesting, as all knew about the ban but tried their luck anyway. Ida Pfeiffer spent a lonely night in an adjacent tower, Harriet Martineau heaped scorn on the inhospitable monks, and Isabel Burton shrugged the rejection aside, since she had a tent.

The women in Martineau's party also camped, in spite of reports of marauding Bedouin. Martineau wrote that "our dragoman lay down at one end of our tent, and the cook at the other, begging us to feel quite secure."[19]

Monks threatened Cristina di Belgiojoso and her party with a large rock precariously balanced on the ramparts above their heads. A group of Englishmen had been recently kicked out for bad behavior, and now everyone was turned away. No letter of recommendation, she concluded, not even one from the tsar, would change the monks' minds.[20]

Belgiojoso, Burton, Emily Beaufort, Martineau, and Bell all preferred tents to vermin-infested khans, but the logistics of camping were formidable. Of the tents, clothes, food, and utensils hauled by Louisa Jebb and X, Jebb wrote, "It all seemed a great deal now, and yet we were only taking necessaries. But then it had been so very hard to know what necessaries were."[21] They miscalculated more often than not and frequently found themselves short of supplies. Jebb believed that their rough travel forced them to confront what was truly important in life:

> You are brought up face to face with something fundamental; all the little accessories with which we have learnt to shield ourselves fall away, and you are just there, stripped yourself, and in the middle of naked realities. And if only you have been wet enough, or cold enough, or hungry enough, it has been worth while, for you never forget it; and the remembrance of it will come to you ever and anon when you are once more tied up in the bonds of convention and are struggling to keep a true idea of what is a reality and what is not.[22]

Few middle- or upper-class European women would have been accustomed to such vagabondage, whether they had traveled widely or not. Those who had been to southern Europe would certainly have been acquainted with vermin, and, because plumbing was unreliable most everywhere, they would have been prepared for malodorous and squalid facilities. These rough conditions forced women to adapt to all inconveniences, not only to dirt and lack of privacy, but to lack of security as well. If they succeeded in banishing squeamishness, their sense of intrepidness grew and gave them confidence, which was in turn rewarded by the respect given to them by their escorts for behaving so unexpectedly stoically.

*Tourist tent camp,*
*Palestine, 1860–1900.*
Photo courtesy Library of Congress
LC-DIG-ppmsca-04960.

By the early nineteenth century, hotels were opening in the major cities; Constantinople had *pensions* by 1813. References in Hester Stanhope's correspondence to two European entrepreneur hoteliers, Mrs Testa and Mme Fontin, date from this time. In the 1840s, Mme Josephine, also called Giuseppina, was a favorite innkeeper.

Austrian Ida Pfeiffer was relieved to find hospitality at Mme Balbiani's Constantinople hotel in 1842.* Pfeiffer had been snubbed by her countrymen despite her letters of introduction, because, she figured, she did not "travel in great pomp or with a great name." Returning in 1848, after her first trip around the world, she was crushed when told Balbiani had retired. She was directed to Aux Quatre Nations, run by a Mme Prust, "a talkative French woman, who was always singing the praises of her housekeeping, servants, cookery, etc., in which, however, none of the travellers agreed with her."[23]

Constantinople's most famous and expensive hotel from

*It is tempting to speculate that Mme Balbiani was, in fact, Mme Josephine, but I have not been able to confirm this.

**CONSTANTINOPLE—PERA.**

## HOTEL DE L'EUROPE,

**Mr. G. N. DESTUNIANO, Proprietor.**

T H I S superior and well-managed
Hotel is admirably situated, and com-
mands a magnificent view of the Bosphorus,
the Harbour, and the Golden Horn.
Gentlemen visiting Constantinople will find
this Establishment excellent in every respect,
and replete with comfort.
Mrs. Destuniano being English is an addi-
tional guarantee that the strictest attention
will be paid to English visitors.

*Hôtel de l'Europe,*
*advertisement, 1871.*

the 1850s to the 1870s was
the Hôtel d'Angleterre, also
called "Missirie's" after its
owner, James Missirie. In the
1860s, this establishment on
the rue de Pera cost U.S.$4,
including board, and smoking was forbidden, the fear of
fire in Constantinople was so
intense. Missirie had two
further claims to fame: in
1835, he had been the dragoman of English traveler
Alexander Kinglake, and he had married an
Englishwoman. Emilia Hornby called Mrs
Missirie "a most kind and excellent person, to
whom every one flies in all the numerous difficulties which
strangers meet with here." Mr G. N. Destuniano, owner of the
Hôtel de l'Europe, had also married an Englishwoman and,
therefore, guaranteed special attention for English guests.[24]

In Damascus, from the early 1840s until about 1860, the only
hotel was the modest but well-liked Dimitri's on the Street
Called Straight. Martineau, Digby, Beaufort, Burton, and Anne
and Wilfrid Blunt all stayed there. Although new hotels opened
after 1860, none were European-style until nearly the end of
the century.

Cairo's famous Shepheard's Hotel opened in the quarter of
the "Franks"★ in the early 1840s, though it wasn't called
Shepheard's until 1846, when Sam Shepheard became its
owner. Its popularity was such that travelers, including Harriet
Martineau, were regularly turned away. So many women opted
to have their babies there that Shepheard griped, "[you'd] think
I keep a lying-in hospital."[25]

---

★The word "Franks" was used in the East to describe all Europeans, no matter the
country of origin.

With the establish-
ment of European-style
hotels, travel became
more democratic,
expanding the world
of travel for an ever-
growing number of
women. Hotels adver-
tised *Salons pour dames*
or noted that families
were especially wel-
come. Women who
would have never
considered traveling
rough in the manner

*Shepheard's Hotel,
advertisement, 1868.*

of Cristina di Belgiojoso or Ida Pfeiffer could
now go to Constantinople or Cairo, at least,
without any qualms.

## DAILY BREAD

*[Arten] was quick, thin, methodical, dirty, intelligent, and untruthful;
he was also the cook. I say the cook advisedly, for a cook he was not . . .
At any rate he knew, being a hungry man himself, that we were in need
of food of some sort at stated intervals.*—Louisa Jebb, 1908[26]

Few travelers were as explicit about the difficulties of provisioning as Louisa Jebb. She and X were constantly stretching
pathetic rations to feed themselves and their men. At one point,
Arten threw their only food—an onion, some chocolate,
Bovril, and rice—into a pot, producing an inedible stew. X
rejected it after one taste and began absentmindedly chewing
on some bread she had stored away. Jebb had seen it before:

I recognised it by a black, burnt mark resembling a figure 8. It had
first appeared on the scene early in the week . . . and with wasteful

squander I had rejected it . . . The men had tried it after me, pinch-
ing it with their grimy fingers, but being unsatisfied with the
consistency they had thrown it, along with other scraps, into a bag
containing miscellaneous cooking utensils. The next day it . . . had
been left on the ground. But as we rode away Hassan's economi-
cal spirit overcame him; he dismounted again and slipped it into
his pocket, where it lay in close proximity to various articles not
calculated to increase the savouriness of its flavour. I was determined to see its end, and when X laid down half—no doubt
meaning it for my share—I threw it on the fire . . .

    The cook picked it out, blew the ashes off, and rubbed it with
his greasy sleeve. He offered it to me.

    "Eat it yourself," I said magnanimously . . . but he wrapped it
carefully in one of the dirty linen bags and put it on one side.

    "Jarin" (To-morrow), he said.[27]

A number of travelers made a point of commenting on the
meals they were offered in harems or by Bedouin. Some never
accustomed themselves to thrusting their fingers into the com-
munal platters of steaming pilaf. Many urged others to bring
their own provisions. For her and her husband's trek through
Syria in 1840, Lady Francis Egerton's list of essential foods
included "portable soup, sea biscuit, pasta, sago, arrowroot,
cheese from England, and tea." *Murray's* recommended a coop
for the chicken that would, naturally, be brought. Isabella Bird,
crossing Bakhtiari country, took no chances with food; she had
already lost thirty-two pounds during the forty-six-day journey
from Baghdad to Teheran. Her supplies included tea, tins of preserved meat and milk, dried soups, and saccharin.[28]

    Women quickly learned, as did their male counterparts, that
dependence on others for food could be a potentially fatal mistake. In this regard, self-reliance proved essential.

If I Had Been a Man

*Sincere or not, pusillanimity is one of the most formidable enemies of*
*the traveler. In the Orient, especially, whoever does not know how to*
*vanquish this painful feeling must be condemned to a sedentary life.*
—Cristina di Belgiojoso, 1855[29]

The difficulties of early travel in the East were largely the result
of differences in culture and language, as well as the extremes of
climate and terrain. But in certain respects, travel here took less
effort than in Europe. Escorts were easily arranged, as were
porters with their pack animals to carry however much luggage
the traveler cared to take. As in Europe, however, the more
money the traveler dispensed, the fewer the inconveniences.

Accidents could happen anywhere, and travelers faced the
same dangers whether in Nice, Naples, or Beirut. Dysentery
and cholera were common, and plague, notable outbreaks of
which swept through the East in 1813–15 and 1835, was especially worrisome.

Prudery, though hardly fatal, was another obstacle. Middle-
and upper-class women demanded a level of privacy rarely
attainable on the road. This requirement must have led to
untold complications with regard to hygiene. Ida Pfeiffer did
not wash or change her clothes for the duration of a ten-day
voyage to Alexandria. To add insult to injury, a curious Greek
sailor stuck her toothbrush in his mouth. Some travelers noted
that they frequently slept in their clothes. Very few explained
just how they went about bathing. Emily Beaufort implied that
she bathed daily in her tin tub, which doubled as a carry box.
Isabella Bird had difficulties finding a place to use her India-
rubber bath. Anne Blunt wrote that she and her husband,
Wilfrid, took occasional baths in their tent but gave no
specifics.

Menopause would have eliminated a major irritant and
handicap, and may be why many women who traveled
through adverse conditions in their later years did so with

much equanimity. However, menstruation, like other intimate topics, was not referred to.

Bird, nearly sixty when she trekked through Persia, took more than her fair share of frightening experiences in stride. She foundered through deep snowbanks, withstood a disastrous caravan collision, felt her heart fail in the extreme cold, had to be dragged off her horse and revived more than once, accepted insults and jeers in small towns, and endured theft and threats. Still, of one khan where she could not lock the door, as it was mostly missing, she was able to write, "How completely under such circumstances one has to trust one's fellow-creatures! . . . I fell asleep, fearing nothing worse than a predatory cat."[30]

The difficulties women experienced often resulted from lack of confidence. Having long nurtured a desire to roam, Ida Pfeiffer never guessed that travel could so undermine her fortitude. That she was the object of much awe would not have helped. In Cyprus, the English consul hastened to meet her, astonished to hear of "a lady possessing sufficient courage to undertake so long and perilous a journey by herself." Pfeiffer was never attacked and never became seriously ill, but the attention she attracted wherever she went was discouraging.[31]

Anxiety about being molested is mentioned only rarely, and it is not until the twentieth century that we read of anything explicit. Freya Stark, in Iraq in her late thirties, questioned why some women would fear for their virtue. She wrote, "I think it rather fatuous to worry over such things when once one is middle aged, but Englishwomen here—quite as old as I am and some more so—seem to expect to be assaulted if they walk ten yards alone in the evening."[32]

It would be misleading to suggest that women could travel in this region, or any other on earth, as freely as a man, and many were the frustrations of being a woman in a man's world. Of her struggles with her crew on her journey through Turkey in 1905, Gertrude Bell wrote, "What my servants needed last night was a good beating and that's what they would have got if I had been a man—I seldom remember being in such a state of suppressed rage!—but as it is I have to hold my tongue and get round them."[33]

Rosita Forbes experienced similar problems but found, as women at times did, that firearms gave some authority. On an expedition into Arabia, she countermanded an order given by her guide, Farraj. When her men hesitated, she drew her revolver and announced, "The man who refuses to march with me goes on a long journey." Farraj raised his rifle, but Forbes fired faster. "He was a good target against the sunset," she wrote. "My first shot grazed his hand; my second sent his Martini [rifle] flying." Her head driver exclaimed, "By Allah, your words are as straight as your bullets."[34]

When Isabella Bird was surrounded by angry, gesturing men armed with sticks and calling her a *kafir,* infidel, she removed her revolver from its holster. She wrote, "I very slowly examined the chambers, though I knew well that all were loaded. This had an excellent effect."[35]

Harriet Martineau, in Syria with a party of English travelers, recounted a near attack when their escort, Sheikh Hussein, thought to save himself some money by smuggling them through another's territory. When that sheikh realized what was happening, he set his men upon Martineau's group:

> The guards were mustered, the camels driven together in a mass, the sheikhs flying about, and giving notice that we were to be attacked by Bedoueens from behind the sandhills. The matchlocks were made ready, and swords and knives looked to. Just at this moment, when I was at the height of expectation of seeing the grandest of Desert sights, an old negro camel-driver ran up, snatched the rein out of my hand, and trotted my camel away.[36]

This attack was thwarted, but Martineau later heard that Hussein was ambushed on his return, and six of his men were killed.

*Alexine Tinne in her house in Cairo.* Émile Bayard, artist. Zurcher and Margollé, *Tour du monde* 22: 1870–71, 297.

## INTO DANGER

*[I want a] sort of little cannon or obusier not exceeding 160 kilos each. It must shoot straight, not in a curve and have exploding balls or shells. With such an implement I ought to go anywhere, I am told, and I wish for this article almost most of all.*—Alexine Tinne, 1869[37]

A few women came perilously close to being murdered; wealthy Dutch traveler Alexine Tinne did not escape such a fate. In July 1864, she was in Cairo, miraculously alive, unfelled by the disease that had killed her mother, Harriet; her aunt, Adriana van Capellen; and their maids, Flora and Anna, during their explorations of the Sudan. Traveling up the Nile—Alexine and Harriet's third trip—deep into the Sudan was an astonishingly ambitious, expensive, and tragic adventure for anyone, let alone women.

Far from being discouraged by these deaths, Alexine left Egypt, sailed the Mediterranean, then settled in Algiers in 1867, with plans to use it as a base for desert travel, an idea she soon abandoned because of constant threats from insurgents. In January 1869, she moved to Tripoli, in present-day Libya, and began planning to cross the Sahara. Her caravan, loaded with supplies and gifts, advertised her immense wealth. Made up of two Dutch sailors, Cornelius Oostmans and Arij Jacobse, and a number of Sudanese and Arabs, it reached the town of Murzuq, about 500 miles south of Tripoli, in early March. Illness forced her to stop there for two months. When she recovered, she went to negotiate the protection of Sheikh Ichnuchen, chief of the Tuareg, and met his nephew, Bu Bekker, who was embroiled in a blood feud with other chiefs.

Tinne was finally well enough to leave Murzuq for Ghat, where she was to meet up with Ichnuchen. On 1 August 1869, her caravan was approached by a small band of Arabs and Tuareg, one of whom was Bu Bekker. He declared that he was to guide her from that point on, but a quarrel broke out when his men tried to seize the weapons from hers. Jacobse attempted to intercede and was pierced by a lance. Alexine stepped in, but a blow from a sword severed her hand. Both she and Oostmans were then shot dead, and her caravan was plundered. Word of the tragedy did not reach her family until 18 August. She was thirty-three.[38]

Fortunately, Alexine Tinne's fate was not common. Most women survived their journeys, and some, like Ida Pfeiffer, learned enough from their discomforts and troubles to prepare them for even more challenging adventures.

Travel through the East in the first half of the nineteenth century, especially, required foresight, money, and time. Escorts and porters could be paid to do much of the work and provisioning, but someone had to hire and organize them. It is probably safe to assume that few travelers would have developed these skills while at home. Most families, even those of the lower middle class, engaged a maid to take care of shopping and other chores. And though many of the women who traveled took maids with them, out of their normal milieu maids often proved to be hindrances rather than assets. The traveler, therefore, had to take control, and, by doing so, she proved time and again her ability to act independently.

## UNPROTECTED FEMALES
Ida Pfeiffer (1797–1858) & Isabella Bird (1831–1904)

*[Miss Dawkins] did not intend, she said, to rival Ida Pfeiffer, seeing
that she was attached in a moderate way to bed and board . . . but
she had no idea of being prevented from seeing anything she wished
to see because she had neither father, nor husband, nor brothers
available for the purpose of escort.*—Anthony Trollope, 1860[39]

The fictional Miss Dawkins, who had made her way from
England to the Pyramids via the pen of Anthony Trollope, was
an "unprotected female," a type of traveler who, by the 1860s,
had proliferated in the East and is still to be found.

This singular wanderer wore black, because it was con-
venient, and was always nicely turned out, if not exactly pretty.
Of an indeterminate age, she was unencumbered
by a husband, and those to whom she attached
herself pitied yet resented her. Trollope portrayed
her as more purposeful and courageous than her
male equivalent. "The unprotected female knows

what she is about; she has something to do and she does it," he observed. She had a modest income, could converse easily on any subject, and "is always to be met with on the Nile; she is quite at home at Constantinople . . . but her head-quarters are perhaps at Jerusalem." He added that "she will not be hindered by her petticoats from seeing what men see, and from enjoying that which Nature seems to bring within a man's reach so easily, but which is so difficult to a woman."[40]

Ida Pfeiffer, beyond doubt the original "unprotected female," had longed to travel ever since she was a girl. An advanced education and an active childhood instilled in her a lively curiosity and sense of adventure, but marriage and children delayed her chance to fulfill her dreams. At the age of forty-five, when her sons were grown, she separated from her husband and set off to the Holy Land armed with the paltry results of twenty years' worth of savings and a handful of letters of introduction to a scattering of Austrian consuls (not all of whom could speak German). Leaving Vienna in March 1842, she embarked on the first of six vessels that would carry her down the Danube and thence to Constantinople. Although not her first trip alone—she had been to northern Italy two years earlier—this one was far more ambitious and introduced her to unexpected discomforts, including the discovery that women traveling second class on the Danube boats were quartered with men. This outrage paled in the light of what she experienced over the next nine months.

Keenly aware of the disadvantages of traveling solo, Pfeiffer joined up with Europeans wherever possible. In Constantinople she talked Barons Charles and Frederick von Buseck and artist Hubert Sattler into letting her go with them to Bursa. They had great misgivings about her company but acquiesced once she assured them she could ride (she couldn't but managed anyway).

Hesitating only briefly when told that plague and revolt were raging in Palestine, Pfeiffer then headed south. Well-wishers cautioned her to disguise herself as a man, but she chose to remain identifiably female, having no illusions that her appearance, somewhat stooped and decidedly petite, would not betray her. In loose blouse and Turkish trousers, she declared that "every where I was treated with respect, and kindness and consideration were frequently shown me merely because I was a woman."[41]

On 17 May 1842, she boarded the *Archduke John,* an Austrian Lloyd steamboat, for a nine-day voyage to Smyrna. Her sense of loneliness and isolation was followed by a firm resolve to enjoy herself:

> Once more I was alone among a crowd of people, with nothing to depend on but my trust in Providence. No friendly sympathetic being accompanied me on board. All was strange. The people, the climate, country, language, the manners and customs—all strange. But a glance upward at the unchanging stars, and the thought came into my soul, "Trust in God, and thou art not alone." And the feeling of despondency passed away, and soon I could once more contemplate with pleasure and interest all that was going on around me.[42]

From Smyrna she sailed to Rhodes, Cyprus, and Beirut. En route, she made the acquaintance of artist and author William Henry Bartlett, who was making drawings for Henry Stebbing's *The Christian in Palestine.* They kept each other company on the long trek to Jerusalem.[43]

Pfeiffer's pious occupations were continually disrupted by congregations who openly stared, so fascinated were they by her presence. In one church, her straw hat caused such a ruckus that the priest asked her to exchange it for a veil. Pfeiffer, not about to suffocate herself, told the "reverend gentleman to inform my fellow-worshippers that this was the first time such a thing had been required of a Frankish woman, and that I thought they would be more profitably employed in looking at their prayer-books than at me."[44]

To visit the Dead Sea and the River Jordan, Pfeiffer again sought male company. She set her sights on a party consisting

of Bartlett, four counts,★ a baron, two
doctors, servants, two sheikhs, and a
bodyguard of twelve. Their consensus was
that a woman would be a burden. At last,
Pfeiffer wrote, "Count Wratislaw took my
part, and said that he had watched me
during our ride from Bethlehem to
Jerusalem, and had noticed that I wanted
neither courage, skill, nor endurance, so
that they might safely take me with
them." The pressure on Pfeiffer to keep
up was intense. When fatigued, she clung
to her horse until the men collapsed;
when ill, she feigned good health.[45]

A Visit to the
Holy Land.

BY MADAME IDA PFEIFFER.
LONDON.
INGRAM COOKE & Co.
1852.

Pfeiffer went on her own to Cairo and
across the desert to Suez. The disease, dirt, poverty,
and rudeness of Egypt were intolerable to her. Yet
once she left Egypt and experienced the insolence
of southern Italy, she recalled the many kind peo-

*Title page from Ida
Pfeiffer's* A Visit to the
Holy Land, *1852.*

ple she had met and admitted that she had been far better treated
than she had realized. She could only conclude that "very few
things [were as she] had imagined them to be."[46]

It is not easy for today's traveler to comprehend just how difficult a trip this was for a single woman. Despite being told how
brave she was and despite her misgivings at the end of her journey, Pfeiffer seemed not to recognize how unusual she was. She
expected to be able to move about freely and, when thwarted,
had the will and determination to persevere. This was superb
training for her subsequent demanding voyages around the
world, the first of which included a daunting trek through
Mesopotamia, and to Madagascar, where imprisonment by
Queen Ranavala, who punished all Christians on the island after
an attempted coup, led to a fatal breakdown in Pfeiffer's health.

---

★The group included Count Berchthold, with whom she later joined forces on the
   Brazil segment of her first journey around the world.

Englishwoman Isabella Bird renounced her customary "unprotected female" status for a good portion of her trip through Mesopotamia and Persia by traveling with Major Herbert Sawyer, "M——" in her *Journeys in Persia and Kurdistan,* whom she introduced as one of "three novelties—a fellow-traveller, a saddle mule, and an untried saddle."[47]

The journey, commencing in Baghdad in January 1890, took the pair to Teheran, and then west again to Bakhtiari country. Sawyer, on a mission for the Indian Army, pushed their team hard through the worst weather the region could produce, but Bird proved a worthy partner. They parted at Borujerd in Lorestan, where Sawyer's mission ended. Her response was joy that "no call to 'boot and saddle' will break the stillness of tomorrow morning!"[48]

Bird's onward travels through Kurdistan and Turkey were as difficult, but were helped greatly by her Persian attendant, Mirza Yusuf, whom she had hired in Teheran, and her loyal and affectionate horse, Boy. She took a large medical kit along with her, and at each village she was swamped with cries for medicines for eye infections, coughs, skin irritations, and bullet

wounds. After having journeyed on horseback for hours, she would sit in her tent, usually in temperatures well over 100°F, attending the sick and wounded; in thanks, she was robbed twice, the second time losing many valuable supplies and notes. She gained expertise on the conditions of the Armenians and spoke on this subject in the House of Commons in 1891.

*"Mrs. Bishop [Isabella Bird] in her travelling dress in Erzeroum," also showing her Persian attendant, Mirza Yusuf (right), Turkish-born Irishman Murphy O'Rourke (left), and Bird's horse, Boy.*

Stoddart, *The Life of Isabella Bird*, 1906, facing p. 242.

Pfeiffer and Bird were unparalleled "unprotected females." But they, like their more commonplace counterparts, risked loneliness. This sentiment overwhelmed Pfeiffer on her journey and was exacerbated by her determination to travel as cheaply as possible. In Bird's case, she was on her ninth significant journey and had become what Trollope called "an old soldier," hardened to the realities of solitary travel.

Loneliness was universal among single women travelers, and it does not take much effort to discover why this should have been so. Unexpected and disapproved of, a woman on her own was isolated in ways most men could never imagine. In European cities, for example, she could not walk alone at night for fear of being mistaken for a prostitute. She could not dine by herself in a restaurant. Some hotels offered a table d'hôte, at which guests sat together, but then some hotels did not accept women on their own. Single women exhausted themselves in sightseeing by day so that they could sleep through interminable nights. Solitude had an even darker side; fear, warranted or not, was magnified out of proportion when there was no one to share it with.[49]

In the East, however, the woman who set aside her own biases and hesitations could easily find hospitality and companionship. Using the common sense that every traveler must cultivate, she would have little reason to feel isolated. Although curious sometimes to alarming degrees, people did not assume that the single woman was immoral and readily invited her into their homes or went out of their way to help her. The stalwart independence that Pfeiffer maintained on her first trip distanced her from chances to overcome her loneliness. She learned from her mistake, and on her subsequent travels, she readily accepted hospitality wherever it was offered.

## JUST ORDINARY GIRLS
Rosita Forbes (1893–1967) & Freya Stark (1893–1993)

*The curly red lines across African deserts had the fascination of a magnet, and I hoped, fervently, that the pioneers, who were writing their names over the blank spaces, would leave just one small desert for me!*—Rosita Forbes, 1928[50]

Englishwoman Rosita Forbes could not help herself. Wherever she went, she raised hackles. Other travelers accused her of fabricating her journeys, officials wrung their hands when she wandered into their territories, bureaucrats despaired of her political interference.

She created a minor sensation in 1920–21 by venturing deep into the Libyan desert to Al-Kufrah, an oasis on the Saharan trade route and

*Rosita Forbes: "The Author as a Beduin sheikh." Forbes, The Secret of the Sahara, 1921, facing p. 2.*

the home of the Senusi, adherents of a movement formed in 1837 to follow the doctrine of pure Islam. Long antagonistic to explorers attempting to survey this portion of the Libyan desert, the Senusi—together with the region's isolation and hostile climate—kept intruders at bay. The first recorded expedition, led by Gerhard Rohlfs, reached the oasis in 1873 but was attacked and its notes and maps looted.

Forbes was accompanied on her trip in 1920 by Oxford-educated Egyptian civil servant Ahmed Hassanein. A letter of recommendation secured by Forbes from Emir Faisal to Sayed Idris, the head of the Senusi at Ajdabiyah, about 125 miles southwest of Benghazi, won them a good reception in November, but Idris's backing alone was insufficient. Knowing that they could expect nothing better, they crept away one freezing night with their guide, Abdullah; two servants, Yusuf and Mohammed; and some Bedouin and Sudanese porters. Forbes transformed herself into Sitt Khadija; Hassanein covered his English-tailored suit with a flowing white shirt and loose trousers. Their shared tent, divided by a "harem" curtain, became a refuge for note taking.[51]

Following two contradictory maps, the pair headed south and quickly ran into trouble: they had brought provisions for two, assuming that the porters would fend for themselves; the porters assumed otherwise and consumed food at an alarming rate. To make things worse, Forbes had a swollen foot and Hassanein suffered from rheumatism. They stumbled into sandstorms and over scattered heaps of bones, animal and human. Their camels sickened, and their water ran out.

A rumor began circulating that Forbes and Hassanein were reconnoitering the oasis for future occupation. When this rumor reached the pair at Buzaymah, they realized their lives were in danger. At the village of Hawari, a few days' march from Al-Kufrah, they were robbed and threatened with death for their perceived treachery. Villagers prevented them from moving on, but they were finally released when Mohammed, who had gone on ahead to present their case to Senusi officials, returned with an unambiguous welcome. Illness and unrest prevented them from visiting any oasis villages other than At Taj and Al-Jawf, the Senusi government and religious center.

Their return trip was worse, even though they took a shorter route. Knowing they would be at least twelve days without water, they had reduced the size of the caravan from eighteen to nine, but their guide lost his way. A bare fifty miles from Siwa, Hassanein fell and broke a clavicle. After several days of slow and painful travel, the group ran into a Camel Corps patrol, which had been sent out to look for them.

Forbes's journey won her few friends among Arabists. Gertrude Bell, for one, belittled Forbes's ability to travel and to speak Arabic and accused her of downplaying Hassanein's role in her book *The Secret of the Sahara*. Hassanein, who returned to Al-Kufrah in 1923, barely acknowledged Forbes in his own book, *The Lost Oases*. Nonetheless, Forbes's account stands as an example of an intrepid journey.

A female journalist may have inadvertently summed up Forbes's handicap in the world of travel. While interviewing her in a mundane hotel room, the reporter looked in vain for some sign of greatness. She then sighed and said, "You must have been a disappointment to many—haven't you? Why, you look just like an ordinary girl."[52]

Much has been written by and about another unremarkable-looking wanderer, Freya Stark. Like Forbes, she was mocked, mostly because of her history of capricious behavior. An illness of questionable severity in the remote Hadhramaut of southern Arabia led to a costly Royal Air Force rescue; her misguided search for antiquities caused her to be ignominiously escorted to the Persian border; she smuggled a car to Teheran from India as a lark, causing a scandal that had to be hushed up; her marriage in middle age to a known homosexual caused tongues to wag and heads to shake. But she produced some twenty-four books of travel and correspondence, all memorable for their zest for adventure. When reading her, it's impossible not to feel that you've been invited along on her travels and that excitement is just around the corner.

Born in Paris to English parents, and having split her youth between Italy and England, with occasional visits to her father in British Columbia, Canada, Stark came to understand that, for her, travel was "escape." She wrote that she was able to shrug aside the duties that most people had to attend to because she was, so she was told, "wild by nature." Her Middle Eastern journeys

*Freya Stark in Arab dress, 1928.* Stark, *Beyond Euphrates*, with permission of John Murray, 1928.

began when she and her friend Venetia Buddicom went from Damascus to Jerusalem in 1927, essentially tracing Gertrude Bell's route through the Hauran. But her experiences in Baghdad in 1929 show how her intrepid spirit, which would have been an asset in earlier days, clashed with the now-established expatriate community there.[53]

Stark had moved to Baghdad with the idea of improving her Arabic. To immerse herself in the language and to save money, she rented a room in the "native" quarter. Outrage from the British was swift and vociferous; she had smeared their reputation and damaged "national prestige." Her mistake revealed to her that she was not in the fascinating and remote land she had imagined but, instead, had landed in the thick of the society she wanted to avoid. In this city, now well populated with her countrymen, the Englishwoman was a mere appendage to her husband or father. She wrote that "this double loss of individuality, inflicted on one-half of the human race, came to me with a shock."[54]

The alternative to her simple lodging, the British Club, excluded Arabs. She thought it a poor thing to be forbidden to associate with the very people she had come to meet. "There was a *Passage to India* feeling for which I had been quite unprepared," she observed, "and half a dozen women told me in a marked way that they had lived in Iraq for a varying number of years 'and never had a *wog* across their doorstep.'" Although she attempted to make amends, she was far too independent to capitulate entirely. Eventually, she befriended the more open-minded and diplomatic Englishwomen.[55]

Stark went to Persia twice between 1930 and 1932, for which she received the Royal Geographical Society Back Memorial Grant and the Royal Asiatic Society Burton Memorial Medal. Some writers, including biographer Molly Izzard, have questioned whether her ability as a self-promoter was more responsible for her honors and recognition than the travels themselves. Stark herself believed "that a woman gets far more than her legitimate share of praise, merely because of her comparative rarity in the explorer's world."[56]

*[I was] very much pleased to learn that all along the road I have been generally mistaken for a boy. I had no idea of any disguise, but as soon as I found it out I encouraged the idea and I shall do so in future whenever we are off the usual beaten tracks.*—Isabel Burton, 1875

# *Dressing* en Amazone
## OVERCOMING DECENCY

ISABEL BURTON shed her cumbersome European trappings and dressed for freedom and comfort, while many of her country-women floundered about in their voluminous dresses. Barely manageable in countries where laundresses, seamstresses, and maids abounded, these complicated garments were a great handicap in the East. Trailing skirts gathered dust; bustles and crinolines inhibited movement; and corsets aggravated the effects of heat. Tight bodices and uplifted bosoms affronted Muslim sensibilities, as did the lack of veils.

Women's accustomed travel attire was designed more for European propriety and style than for practicality. The alternatives, however, were almost too radical. Wouldn't it be indecent of a woman to wear an "Amazone," a divided skirt, even if it was essential for riding? Could a woman still be feminine while swaggering about in tall boots? But if women did not adopt clothing that facilitated travel, the only other option was seclusion and discomfort.

The wearing of Oriental clothing by Europeans has been the subject of debate among scholars of Orientalism. European men, especially, who dressed "native" have been criticized for indulging their fantasies and for disguising themselves to infiltrate societies they wished to conquer. But

*Jane Dieulafoy: "Two days in the rain under an Arab tent." Myrbach, engraver, after a photo. Dieulafoy, Tour du monde 55: 1887, 25.*

*English dressed as Afghanis for a fancy-dress party, c. 1890. The Orient was a favorite theme for costumes throughout the nineteenth century and into the twentieth.* Unidentified photographer.

they have also been defended for taking care to conform to local customs and laws.

Up to the mid-nineteenth century, there were several reasons why a foreigner might adopt the apparel of a region. Conforming meant greater acceptance and less attention. Travelers compared themselves to someone from the East dressing as a Westerner to avoid attracting stares and murmurs on the Champs-Élysées or Oxford Street. More important, during the rule of certain Ottoman sultans— Murad IV (reigned 1623–40), Abdulhamid I (r. 1774–88), and Selim III (r. 1788–1807), for example—laws were passed forbidding anyone to wear European clothing. Murad had offenders beheaded. Eastern clothing was also more comfortable than European attire, having been adapted to suit the climate.[1]

Most women saw the sense of modifying their clothing to make it less restrictive, but even then they found themselves at odds with their surroundings. Amelia Edwards mockingly described herself and her friend Lucy as "sorry figure[s] with our hideous palm-leaf hats, green veils, and white umbrellas." Edwards's bizarre outfit was the Europeans' idea of suitable attire for low latitudes. Emily Beaufort, who exhorted women to leave their "crinoline in Cairo" before heading off to the Pyramids, made a few other practical suggestions, but soberly assumed that women would continue to wear dresses.[2]

Women with more sense than style adopted or modified local garments or European men's clothing and discovered that increased comfort and ease of circulation permanently changed their attitude to dress and how they saw themselves.

*Tourists in Jerusalem, 1860–90.* Photo courtesy Library of Congress LC-USZ62-104825.

## Dressing as an Eastern Woman

*If you are in a room be of the same colour as the people in it.*
—Persian proverb quoted by Ella Sykes, 1901[3]

Traditional Eastern women's outdoor dress in the nineteenth century depended on the region and the occasion but generally consisted of loose trousers worn under a long-sleeved robe, covered by a cloak, headdress, and veil. Much of this clothing is still worn today, with some modifications. Head coverings range from

*"Women of Latakia, Syria." The one on the right wears a* yashmak *and* feradge *and smokes a* nargileh. *E. Zier, artist. Lortet, Tour du monde 39: 1880, 167.*

the *hejab,* or head scarf, to the all-concealing Persian *chador.* Until the 1880s, married Druze women of Lebanon also wore on their heads a tall metal pillar known as a *tantur.* In Turkey, travelers would have noticed the *yashmak*—a flattering semi-transparent veil of white gauze—and the *feradge,* a shapeless cloak that covered the entire body.

Christian and Jewish women wore variations on these outfits; many living in towns and cities conformed to some degree to the practice of veiling in public. In rural areas, women of all religions who tended the land followed fewer dress restrictions and rarely veiled themselves.

Lady Mary Wortley Montagu enjoyed wearing the sumptuous, corsetless Turkish clothing. One complimentary white and gold outfit consisted of damask and brocaded pantaloons, kid leather shoes, a silk gauze smock, a damask waistcoat, and a bro-caded caftan, over which was placed an exquisitely embroidered girdle; a loose robe went on top of the girdle. A headdress made up of a cap and tassel completed the ensemble. To roam freely and "to gratify a passion that is become so powerful with me as curiosity," Montagu wore a *yashmak*. By today's standards, this outfit seems excessive and constrictive, but in comparison with early eighteenth-century European corsets, petticoats, and extravagant headdresses, she was simply clad. She did not sacrifice her femininity by wearing this apparel, and in it she emulated Turkish women, whom she considered to be "perhaps more free than any ladies in the universe."[4]

*Lady Mary Wortley Montagu in Turkish dress.* W. Greatbatch, artist. Montagu, The Letters of Lady Mary Wortley Montagu, 1837, vol. 1, frontispiece.

By the late 1700s, Western women habitually donned local female dress when in cities. Eliza Fay, en route to India with her new husband, wrote of her brief sojourn in Cairo in 1779. She was obliged to wear trousers, boots, a belted satin gown, a short-sleeved robe, and a muslin headdress covered by a silk robe and veil and then by a length of black silk. The twenty-three-year-old Fay thought it "a terrible fashion for one like me, to whom free air seems the great requisite for existence," but she tolerated it in order to tour the city.[5]

Lady Mary Elgin lived in Constantinople from 1799 until 1802 with her ambassador husband, Lord Thomas Bruce Elgin. She delighted in fooling him by disguising herself in a priceless Turkish woman's ensemble, given to her by the sister of the "captain pasha." To her mother, she wrote, "All the women said I was excessively like the Sultan's favorite . . . they all flocked round me when I returned to them, to know what E[lgin] thought of them."[6]

French poet and diplomat Alphonse de Lamartine and his wife, Marianne-Elisa, originally Miss Birch from Britain, traveled through Syria in 1832 and 1833. As Damascenes were still antagonistic toward foreigners, the couple were smuggled into the city, she having been "wrapped from head to foot in a long veil of white cloth." After this intriguing start, her visit there must have been very tedious. Alphonse, who left her in her lonely room while he went about with their host, M. Baudin, met many Armenian women in the course of his visits to homes and confessed, "I couldn't tear my eyes away from these striking women." One imagines him entertaining his wife with vivid descriptions of their charms.[7]

Midway through their travels, their young daughter, Julia, died. Devastated, Alphonse abandoned his journal for four months. When he resumed it, he recalled how Julia had liked to dress up: "Her mother braided her long, blond curls in imitation of the women of Beirut, arranged her shawl into a turban and placed it on her head. I had never seen anything more delightful . . . than the face of Julia, crowned thus with the turban of Aleppo."[8]

Scottish painter Sir David Wilkie visited Syria and Turkey in 1840. While there he made several sketches of Mrs Moore, the wife of the Beirut consul, and of popular Constantinople innkeeper Mme Josephine, but only after they agreed to dress in Eastern costume for him. Whether they wore this clothing as a matter of course, however, is not known.

*"Mrs Moore, wife of the British Consul at Beyrout in an Arab Dress," 1841.*
Wilkie, *Sir David Wilkie Sketches*, 1843, pl. 13.

Harriet Martineau, in rejecting Egyptian garments, found herself barely able to withstand

the attention she attracted, especially at villages along the Nile. "The staring was not rude or offensive," she admitted, "but it was enough to be very disagreeable; at least, to one who knew, as I did, that the appearance of a woman with an uncovered face is an indecency." To her, it was the hardest part of travel in the East, yet she advised others to follow suit, as she believed one must be proud of one's own customs. But she also noted that dirt and dust clung to the hems of their dresses.[9]

Martineau's 1846–47 trip up the Nile to Abu Simbel was, by then, fairly routine, but an expedition to Palmyra, in Syria, was still dangerous in 1853. Jane Digby and her maid, Eugénie, went there attired as Bedouin men for safety's sake, as their escort was not about to guarantee protection if it became known they were European.

After her marriage to Medjuel al-Mezrab, Digby wore modified Bedouin women's clothing when in the desert. At home in Damascus, she would don a plain shift, adding a veil over her nose and mouth for receiving male visitors. She also dyed her light-brown hair black and braided it. According to Isabel Burton, "[Digby] led a semi-European life. She blackened her eyes with kohl, and lived in a curiously untidy manner. But otherwise she was not in the least extraordinary."[10]

While in Damascus, Isabel Burton wore a variety of Eastern outfits. For the city she favored an "izár, to walk about the bazars *incognita* like a native. It covers all, except your face, from head to foot, like a shroud." Visits to the *hammam,* or bath, called for baggy linen trousers, tight at the ankle, and a robe gathered at the neck, belted at the waist, and falling to the knees. Added to this were yellow slippers, a turban, jewelry, a long white lace veil for the front, and a broad one that fell down the back.[11]

Burton emphasized clothing in *The Inner Life of Syria,* perhaps aware that her women readers would be more enraptured by that subject than by another favorite topic, her husband, Richard.

## DRESSING AS A MAN

*They think how happy we are*
*to dress like men, and follow*
*our husbands like comrades.*
—Isabel Burton, 1875[12]

Women today wear trousers
with little thought to what
that entailed in the past. The
opposition to women wear-
ing male garments was fierce
on the part of both men and
women. Even those most
basic of items, underpants,
were rejected until the introduction of the crinoline in
1856, which could and did
fly up revealingly. Before
then, the resistance to draw-
ers or knickerbockers, as
they were called in Britain,
came from the fact that they
were men's clothing; rare
female wearers of such—
actresses and lesbians, for
instance—had been considered depraved.

*Jane Dieulafoy in Persia.*
Émile Bayard, artist. Dieulafoy, *Tour du*
*monde* 44: 1883, 137.

In France, from 1789 until 2004, a trouser-clad
woman was a law breaker. In the 1830s, the Saint-
Simoniennes were mocked for the pantaloons
peeking out from under their skirts. Fifty years
later, archaeologist Jane Dieulafoy, who traveled through Persia
dressed as a man, needed a *Permission de travestisement,* Permit to
Cross-Dress (granted by the police in case of health or occupa-
tional requirements) and indulged in the opportunity to dress
comfortably even while in Paris. According to the London

*French actress Rachel*
*dressed as Roxane for the*
*play* Bazajet *by Racine,*
*c. 1838.* Achille Devéria, artist.
Gauthier, *Achille et Eugène Devéria*, 1925.

*Times,* she wore trousers to escort the shah of Persia through the Louvre in 1889.[13]

In Britain, rigorous social disapproval kept women in skirts. As the French journalists had had a field day with the Saint-Simoniennes, so did the British and American press when Elizabeth Cady Stanton and Amelia Bloomer introduced the bloomer in 1850–51, inspired by trouser-clad American Elizabeth Smith Miller. Supporters of bloomers soon abandoned the style, however, when they realized that their clothes were getting more attention than feminist issues. Bloomers took over forty years to catch on, when they were adopted for bicycle wear.

Western women traveling in the East were of two minds about male attire, even if it meant greater comfort and security. They had long been taught that it was indecent to reveal the shape of the leg, and they feared disapproval from both men and women for usurping this symbol of masculinity. But when in the East, many saw how this simple change in attire would open up their world and realized that outside certain enclaves there were few compatriots around to take issue with them.

The sight of a woman wearing men's clothing would have been completely unexpected in the early to mid-nineteenth century, so it is no wonder that women were able to occasionally pull off the disguise. Even when Eastern men saw through it, however, to question a woman's outfit would have been unthinkably rude. This reticence no doubt led many women to believe they had succeeded in deluding everyone.

Mary Elgin was excited by the opportunity to accompany her husband to audiences with the Turkish grand vizier and the sultan, since guests were given furs as tokens of their visits. What thrilled her even more, though, was the requirement that she dress as a man. Her regalia consisted of a riding habit, a great-coat with epaulets, and a round beaver hat. At another audience, she wore a fez, pantaloons, and red slippers. Her maid, Masterman, was likewise bedecked.

I can find no record that Elgin was depicted in these clothes, but several dubious portraits of Lady Hester Stanhope in male attire embellish Charles Meryon's *Memoirs* and *Travels of Lady Hester Stanhope*. Meryon, Stanhope's personal physician, made much of her ladyship's apparel:

> In addition to her more splendid habiliments, Lady Hester had, whilst at Cairo, procured a traveling Mameluke [Mamluk]★ dress. It consisted of a satin vest, with long sleeves, open to the bend of the arm, which reached to the hips only, and folding over at the chest was attached with a single button at the throat and waist; over this again she wore a red cloth jacket, in shape like a scanty spencer, with short sleeves, and trimmed with gold lace. The trowsers were of the same cloth, gorgeously embroidered with gold at the pockets, as well before as behind. They were large and loose, as is the fashion in Turkey, and, when worn, formed, by their numerous folds, a very beautiful drapery. Over the whole, when on horseback, she wore the burnooz or white-hooded cloak, the pendent tassels and silky look of which gave great elegance to her figure. The turban was a Cashmere shawl, put on with the peculiar fulness which the Mamelukes affect in their headdress, and which is very becoming.
>
> She was generally mistaken for some young bey with his musta-chios not yet grown; and this assumption of the male dress was a subject of severe criticism among the English who came to the Levant.[14]

---

★The Mamluks were a military class of political importance in Egypt until Muhammad 'Ali had a large number of them massacred in 1811.

Stanhope herself wrote, "I liked Egypt extremely, notwith-standing the narrow streets, the stinks, and bad eyes; but had I been dressed as a woman I should not have liked it at all, for I should not have seen anything."★[15]

Stanhope advised Lady Juliana Belmore, heading to Egypt in 1817, to wear a veil, in order that she be "admired and consid-ered the wife of a great Pasha, for it is quite impossible to say how the Turks in Syria are *horrified* with European costume." And she rigorously enforced the dress of her maids Anne Fry and Elizabeth Williams,★★ whether Bedouin male clothing for travel or veils in the manner of local women for circulating through towns and cities.[16]

Meryon described Mrs Fry's attempts to go about in mascu-line dress as singular failures. "From her timidity in this new garb . . . [she] was often exposed to the danger of falling from her ass, on which she persisted in sitting in the decorous pos-ture customary with women in England: although in a country where women invariably ride astride, and where there are no side saddles, she might have imitated them with less singularity and without indecency."[17]

Stanhope's standards of male dress apparently did not apply to other women. Historian Henri d'Allemagne recounts how a group of Saint-Simoniens, including Clorinde Rogé clad in Eastern male attire, tried to visit Stanhope in 1836. A servant met them at the door, saying that "Lady Stanhope was furious to have learned that a woman in men's clothing had dared to enter her house, and that in consequence, there was nothing for them but to leave."[18]

Saint-Simonienne Suzanne Voilquin was required to wear

---

★This impression was echoed almost a hundred years later, when Algeria traveler Isabelle Eberhardt declared that "dressed as a young European woman I would never have seen anything; the world would have been closed to me, for external life seems to have been made for man and not for woman."[19]

★★Anne (or Ann) Fry stayed with Stanhope until around 1814. Xenophobic, she managed to remain civil by mutating such names as Philippaki into Philip Parker and Mustapha into Mr Farr. Williams had been Stanhope's maid in England and rejoined her mistress in 1816.[20]

Egyptian clothing when working at a Cairo hospital in 1835. Her appearance was that of a gentleman, with bouffant trousers cinched in by a wide belt and tucked into high boots, complemented by a short vest and a white wool cloak, known as a burnous. On her head sat a fez, in her belt was a saber. The costume may have seemed like masquerade, but it allowed her to earn money to survive.[21]

Emily Beaufort, in Syria with her sister in 1859, dismissed the idea of wearing men's clothing, but their travel attire nonetheless incorporated Arab men's cloaks. She credited these with fooling would-be bandits into thinking their party was stronger than it was. Firearms gave the robbers added incentive to desist. "The fun of the thing," Beaufort admitted, "was, that, though we all showed our pistols and revolvers, not one of us, even the dragomans, had remembered to re-load them on leaving Damascus."[22]

For traveling cross-country, Isabel Burton wore a modified riding habit that she described as "a very decent compromise between masculine and feminine attire." She stuck a revolver and a knife into a leather belt, hid her hair under a fez, then draped herself with a keffiyeh, the scarf still worn today. With her shape concealed in this manner, she could "go into all the places which women are not deemed worthy to see, and receive all the respect and consideration that would be paid to the son of a great man."[23]

Burton believed she was mistaken for Richard's son (unlikely, as she was stout and nearly forty) and vowed to dress accordingly whenever heading to remote areas, arguing that "wild people in wild places would feel but little respect or consideration for a Christian woman with a bare face, whatever they may put on of outward show." She acknowledged that city residents had become used to European women, but still, "according to their notions, we ought to be covered up and stowed far away from the men, with the baggage and beasts." It seemed that the more convinced she was of this perception, the stronger her determination to defy it.[24]

*Anne and Wilfrid Blunt.*
G. Vuillier, artist. Blunt, *Tour du monde* 43:
1882, 9.

Burton frequented harems in Damascus, dressing in Eastern costume to do so. When, on occasion, she arrived in her riding habit, she was told how like a man she was. Burton declined offers of dresses that would please her husband. "Think of me," she exclaimed, "sitting on a mud floor, *decolletée* in blue tulle and roses, all alone in my eyrie in the Anti-Lebanon, doctoring the poor, and shooting wild game."[25]

At a village en route to Palmyra, local women spied on Burton as she dressed: "I could see fifty pairs of eyes at fifty chinks in the windows and doors. Dressing *en Amazone* seemed to afford them infinite glee, and when I arrived at the cloth nether garments of my riding-habit, they produced shouts of laughter."[26]

Anne Blunt, whose travels in the East with her husband, Wilfrid, began in 1877, wore a modified Bedouin outfit for crossing the Syrian and Arabian deserts. This consisted of simply throwing a robe over her usual coat and adding a keffiyeh. Of their 1879 expedition to the Nejd, she wrote that neither she nor Wilfrid believed they could effectively disguise themselves but wished "to avoid attracting more notice than was necessary." Her reluctance to renounce her English garments was overcome later, while living in Cairo. Gertrude Bell spent an afternoon with her at her home, Sheykh Obeyd, and noted that Blunt wore "full Bedouin costume."[27]

Isabella Bird's travels through Iraq in 1890 were reminiscent of accounts of earlier travel in Syria, when European women were rare. In the bazaars of Kut al Imara, Bird became alarmed when "crowds pressed and followed, picking at my clothes, and singing snatches of songs which were not complimentary. It had not occurred to me that I was violating rigid custom in appearing in a hat and gauze veil rather than in a *chadar* [*sic*] and face cloth, but the mistake was made unpleasantly apparent."[28]

*Rosita Forbes, before and after her adoption of desert travel attire.* Forbes, *The Secret of the Sahara,* 1921, facing p. 22.

Bird had begun wearing bloomers under her riding skirt twenty years earlier for her travels through Hawaii and the United States and also wore them on this trip, but for the glacial Persian winter conditions, she piled on even more:

> Over my riding dress, which is of flannel lined with heavy home-spun, I had a long homespun jacket, an Afghan sheepskin coat, a heavy fur cloak over my knees, and a stout "regulation" waterproof to keep out the wind. Add to this a cork helmet, a fisherman's hood, a "six-ply" mask, two pairs of woollen gloves with mittens and double gauntlets, and the difficulty of mounting and dismounting for a person thus *swaddled* may be imagined![29]

Twentieth-century traveler Gertrude Bell made few alterations to her dress. She adopted a kind of loose turban as protection from the sun and wore a split skirt for riding astride. She traveled rough through all kinds of conditions yet maintained a strict decorum in appearance and bearing, because she believed that her stature as an important personage would protect her and facilitate her travels, and because she thought that "a woman can never disguise herself effectually."[30]

Freya Stark was bluntly criticized by explorer Wilfrid Thesiger for wearing Arab attire. Thesiger, who seemed not to understand the difficulties of traveling in women's clothing, was quoted as saying, "There she is dressed as a man with a dagger and cartridge-belt and a rifle and all the rest of it—well why? If she'd wanted to dress like an Arab she should have worn woman's clothes instead of this ridiculous thing of dressing up like a man or boy—that condemns her from start to finish."[31]

Few travelers were so naive as to think they would be able to wear their comfortable travel clothing in the streets of their own cities. Jane Dieulafoy's persistence in the wearing of trousers in Paris regularly drew more comment than her achievements.

The growth in women's travel throughout the nineteenth century coincided with a general increase in women's participation in hiking, walking, hunting, tennis, bicycling, and golf. Clothing at home was naturally changing to accommodate these activities, and, as early as the 1860s, a complaint sounded that all the pretty girls, with their relatively short riding habits and masculine-detailed jackets, had been "transformed into guys."[32]

There were setbacks, however, such as the enormous bustle of the 1870s, narrow hobble skirts of the 1870s and '80s, and a return to tight lacing in the 1890s. Not until couturiers threw out stays and incorporated trousers into their designs in the second decade of the twentieth century would the average woman dare to wear such apparel in public, and even then, the controversy was intense.

## AN ICONOCLAST
### Lady Hester Stanhope (1776–1839)

Wealthy aristocrat Lady Hester Stanhope, the product of an unorthodox upbringing, spent several years in a position of influence with her uncle, British prime minister William Pitt, before leaving for the East.

Devastated by the deaths of her uncle in 1806 and of her beloved and possibly affianced Sir John Moore two years later, thirty-four-year-old Stanhope, struggling with a £1,200 pension granted by the government, fled England in

*Lady Hester Stanhope had apparently refused to be painted, so portraits of her are suspect.* Attributed to R. J. Hamerton. Hamel, *Lady Hester Lucy Stanhope*, 1913, frontispiece.

February 1810. She sailed to Gibraltar, accompanied by her brother James, her maid, Elizabeth Williams, and her token medical presence, Dr Charles Meryon. It's mainly from Meryon's accounts that we know so much of her life in the East.

In Gibraltar, Stanhope first met Michael Bruce, a twenty-one-year-old on his Grand Tour. Meeting again in Malta, they became lovers and traveled together to Constantinople. Miss Williams, remaining in Malta, was replaced by Mrs Anne Fry.

Stanhope filled her eight-month stay at Constantinople touring and hobnobbing with diplomats. Invited to board the Turkish vessel *Sultan Selim,* she responded with great élan to the condition that she wear men's clothes. This effrontery, along with her brazen liaison with Michael, provoked disapproval from the British plenipotentiary, Stratford Canning, with whom she had developed a friendship.

Stanhope and her entourage left for Egypt in October 1811. Their ship foundered off the coast of Rhodes and most of their belongings—clothes, money, supplies—sank. Out of necessity, Stanhope donned Turkish men's attire, variations of which she wore from that point on, and the voyage resumed. The party landed at Alexandria in January 1812, then headed on to Cairo, where she charmed Egyptian viceroy Muhammad 'Ali with her aristocratic manner and extravagant Tunisian garb.★[33]

From Egypt they sailed to Jaffa, then toured the Holy Land. Stanhope—no doubt still aglow from her sensational Cairo debut—dared to enter Damascus unveiled. Reputedly fanatical crowds watched her procession, either too stunned or too curious to muster their famed hostility. She declared this to be the "most singular and not one of my least exploits."[34]

From her lodgings near the Umayyad Mosque in the Turkish quarter, Stanhope pursued plans to go to Palmyra, once ruled by legendary Queen Zenobia, where no European

---

★Meryon appraised her cashmere turban and girdle at £50 each, gold-embroidered pantaloons at £40, and waistcoat and fur at £50. Stanhope's saber, saddle, and other accoutrements added £155. The total, £295, is estimated at 2002 values to be worth roughly £10,000, or U.S.$16,000.

woman had visited since Roman times. Meryon believed that aside from wishing to see the spectacular ruins, Stanhope "sought the remains of Zenobia's greatness."[35]

The expedition was escorted by Mahannah al-Fadel, a sheikh of the Anazeh, a Bedouin tribe that controlled the routes to Palmyra. On 20 March 1813, Stanhope and Mrs Fry dressed as Bedouin and began the five-day ride, accompanied by Bruce, Meryon, dragomans, valets, grooms, horsemen, and escorts. According to Stanhope, there were forty camels for supplies; Bruce claimed there were seventy. Because her sex and rank were already much celebrated, she decided to travel openly, unlike previous visitors, who had gone in disguise.

The desert bustled with activity; everyone wanted to see this Englishwoman. Her arrival at Palmyra was greeted with great celebration; to Stanhope it was as though she had been acclaimed queen. Although they intended to stay for six weeks, threat of attack sent them back after only a few days.

Word of Stanhope's triumph at Palmyra quickly spread across Syria and to England, in part because of the expense. Her costs for her bodyguard, coffee, tobacco pipes, and gifts came to £1,000.*[36]

Shortly after the Palmyra expedition, Bruce left for England. Between bouts of plague, Stanhope's entourage traveled to Latakia, Baalbek, and Sidon, then to Mar Antonius, a Maronite monastery off-limits to females, a prohibition that Meryon thought provoked Stanhope to visit. She rode her she-ass into the hall and hosted a dinner for the unnerved monks.

After a disastrous attempt to find buried treasure at the ruins of the coastal town of Ascalon in 1815, Stanhope settled briefly at Mar Elias. Mrs Fry left for England in 1816, and in January 1817 Dr Meryon, too, escaped. Stanhope moved to Djoûn, another abandoned monastery near Sidon, where her health, never perfect, declined further. She buried herself in a strange

---

*Approximately £33,750 in 2002 values. Meryon had managed with £10 on his reconnaissance trip.

*Dr Charles Meryon in Arab clothing.* Portrait originally printed in his *Travels of Lady Hester Stanhope,* vol. 3, 1846. Hamel, *Lady Hester Lucy Stanhope,* 1913, facing p. 240.

world of fortune telling, prophesying her entry into Jerusalem, riding alongside the anticipated Messiah, each on a mysteriously marked horse that had been born in her stables. Her wandering stopped, and the world began making its way to her.

Many Europeans, Arabs, and Ottomans visited her at Djoûn, at times swelling the household uncontrollably, as when a troop of Albanians sought refuge from the wrath of Egypt's Muhammad 'Ali. The viceroy, by means of his son, Ibrahim Pasha, had invaded Syria and had made himself the de facto ruler there. But even his authority ended at Stanhope's door. Her interference in local affairs, however, pushed her into a dangerous rivalry with her former ally, the Druze emir Beshir Shihab.

Miss Williams died of a fever in 1828. Stanhope commanded Meryon, now married, to return, but his wife was in no hurry to make such a trip or to let her husband go alone. The couple only succeeded in reaching Djoûn in December 1830. He endured entire nights of Stanhope's ceaseless rambles about past illuminati and future prophets, then left again in the spring.

By now, Stanhope was living in abject poverty, yet she continued to maintain an extravagant household. Then, as if her financial situation weren't wretched enough, her pension was commandeered to pay her outstanding debts. She had frequently resolved to leave Syria, and though she swore she'd never again live in England, she preoccupied herself with its affairs and wrote scathing diatribes, lashing men of power with her opinions of their conduct.

Meryon rejoined her in Djoûn briefly in the summer of 1837, this time with his wife and daughter. At some point in 1839, Stanhope had her house walled up and, as far as anyone can ascertain, lived alone for several months. She died on 23 June 1839. American missionary William McLure Thomson, who officiated over her funeral, summed her up as "wholly and magnificently unique." Thomson bought some of her books and entertained himself with the caustic comments she had written in the margins.[37]

Stanhope's many visitors—James Silk Buckingham, Alphonse de Lamartine, Prince Hermann Pückler-Muskau, and Alexander Kinglake—echoed Meryon's extravagant descriptions, but it is questionable to what degree these accounts of her are accurate. Meryon was in awe of her but also suffered her insults and ingratitude. Knowing this, his fulsome flattery of her regal bearing, stamina, and influence reads as a good dose of irony. He praised her incessant schemes for making the best use of her intellect. In 1815, for example, she conceived a never-fulfilled plan to create an institute of European literary, scientific, and artistic men, who would flood the Ottoman Empire in lofty pursuits.

As the first European woman to travel to Palmyra, Stanhope was venerated; for her superstitions and her isolation in an abandoned monastery, she was dismissed as a crackpot; for her candidness and her defiance of the status quo, she was respected. And as long as her purse remained bottomless, she was worshipped.

*"Why do you work? Are you poor?"*—Question asked of Jane Dieulafoy in Persia, 1881

# More Than Occupied
## SCHOLARLY TRAVEL

THE EAST ATTRACTED numerous learned women, whether traveling solo or in company, who were highly motivated to work and not for money. These women included Jane Dieulafoy, Amelia Edwards, Anne Blunt, and Gertrude Bell, who combined scholarly pursuits with photography, painting, horse breeding, and politics, respectively. Isabel Burton, another much-occupied traveler, though an enthusiastic partner in her husband's career, did not distinguish herself through her own achievements. All managed to deflect the criticism that was focused on another group, the bluestockings, women whose intellectual and literary aspirations earned them disdain from male contemporaries.

### AHEAD OF HER TIME

*[Friends] urged me heartily to stay home. They painted the most attractive pleasures in glowing colours. One day I could put perfumed soaps into the wardrobes, I could create new kinds of marmalades and sauces; the next day I could be supreme head in a battle against flies, hunt for moths, I could darn socks . . . The afternoons would be devoted to the sermons of preachers of fashion, to the offices of the cathedral and to the delicate conversations between women where,*

*Female tourist heading into the Bulak museum. Wilhelm Gentz, artist. Ebers, L'Égypte, vol. 2, 1883, 48.*

*Jane Dieulafoy, c. 1886.*
Dronsart, 1894, 54.

*after having slit the throats of their closest, they refresh themselves in chatter about toilettes, pregnancies and breastfeeding. I knew how to resist all of these temptations.*—Jane Dieulafoy, 1887[1]

Of the women featured here, Jane Dieulafoy was the most modern in outlook, assumptions, and activities, even by today's standards. She formed a partnership with her husband, in work and travel, the equality of which surpasses that of any of the other married women in this book. Between 1881 and 1886, Jane made three expeditions to Persia with her husband, Marcel. Her advance preparations—learning Farsi and studying Persian history and Islamic architecture—qualified her to participate knowledgeably in examinations of the country's monuments and in excavations at the archaeological site of Susa. Admirer Vita Sackville-West, who traveled to Persia in 1926, believed "it was not so much she who accompanied her husband as her husband who accompanied her."[2]

During their first trip, the Dieulafoys surveyed the country's ruins from the Black Sea to the Persian Gulf. Jane concentrated on photography, note taking, and camp organization. To circumvent the prohibition against women appearing publicly, she dressed as a man. Their second expedition was spent at Susa. After briefly returning to France, they went back for another season. She received the Legion of Honor for her work and notoriety for dressing as she pleased.

Jane's accounts, illustrated with engravings from her photographs and Marcel's sketches, were published in the French journal *Le Tour du monde* and in her book *La Perse, la Chaldée et la Susiane*. Fascinating and informative, her writing is also unexpectedly amusing. On one occasion, upon noticing a field of plaster mounds, she asked her guide what the mounds signified. She was told how six brigands had been suspended alive in pits that were slowly filled with the plaster. The guide noticed her expression of horror. "You disapprove?" he asked, then nodded. "You're right. It was a shame to waste so much plaster."[3]

Sackville-West related a friend's childhood memory of attending a Parisian party at which her father pointed out a new arrival. "[I] saw a little grizzled old gentleman," recalled the friend, "in a smoking-jacket, with the Legion of Honour in his buttonhole. 'That', said my father, 'is Madame Dieulafoy.'"[4]

## A PAINTERLY SCHOLAR

*I could have breakfasted, dined, supped on Temples. My appetite for them was insatiable, and grew with what it fed upon. I went over them all. I took notes of them all. I sketched them every one.*
—Amelia Edwards, 1877[5]

When forty-two-year-old Amelia Edwards and her companion, Lucy Renshaw, sailed up the Nile in the winter of 1873–74, Edwards was an established writer. She claimed she went to Egypt solely to get out of England's rain, but, even so, she was probably more intellectually prepared than any woman who had gone there before her. Edwards's nearly complete lack of interest in domestic life propelled her into male territory, that of writing a travel account fortified with scholarly fact. Absorbing and authoritative, *A Thousand Miles Up the Nile* is a landmark in women's travel writing that can be read and reread for the learning, the travel details, and the author's personality. Edwards effortlessly made oft-described subjects fresh and new. Nothing and no one escaped her notice, and she freely admitted how often her preconceived notions were altered by reality. In spite of her humble introduction, "My testimony may not be

"Cleaning the colossus."
Woodcut of Amelia
Edwards's sketch. Edwards, A
Thousand Miles Up the Nile, 1877, 451.

of much value; but I give it for the little that it is worth," she was praised for her erudition.[6]

A gifted watercolorist, Edwards devoted much of her time in Egypt to drawing, and her sketches furnished the illustrations for her book. She was not unusual; sketching and watercolor painting were as natural to the nineteenth-century traveler as journal writing, and travel was perfect for nurturing artistic skills. The artist, aspiring or proficient, once out of the gaze of her society, had more liberty to paint what she wished, even though crowds might gather to watch her. Travel being slower, as well, meant that she could devote more time to a scene. Edwards, for instance, having no pressing cares to interfere, absented herself from her companions for long stretches to draw temples. This isn't to say that pencil and watercolor sketching was always easy.

She described her attempts to capture the grandeur of Ramses II's temple at Abu Simbel:

> [The sand] fills your hair, your eyes, your water-bottles; silts up your colour-box; dries into your skies; and reduces your Chinese white to a gritty paste the colour of salad-dressing. As for the flies, they have a morbid appetite for water-colours. They follow your wet brush along the paper, leave their legs in the yellow ochre, and plunge with avidity into every little pool of cobalt as it is mixed ready for use. Nothing disagrees with them; nothing poisons them—not even olive-green.[7]

*Amelia Edwards.*
After a photograph by F.R. Window.
Dronsart, 1894, 323.

When Andrew McCallum ("the Painter" on the *Philae*) discovered a half-buried doorway at Abu Simbel, Edwards threw herself into the excavation of what turned out to be a chapel. The thrill of this find further encouraged her already strong interest in Egyptology. Back home, after undertaking a series of lectures on Egypt and writing the scholarly *Pharaohs, Fellahs and Explorers,* 1891, she became cofounder of the Egypt Exploration Fund and of the School of Egyptology at the University of London. In an essay on Edwards's travels, Patricia O'Neill wrote that "with the authority that came from having learnt and written about Egypt, Edwards was able to give impetus to the admission of women in to the previously masculine realms of scholarship and cultural authority in the late Victorian period." O'Neill credits her with creating interest in history among women in both Britain and America.[8]

## THE RELUCTANT AUTHOR

*It is very tiresome that everyone fancies I am a writer. I shouldn't mind only I can't do it, and nobody believes one's explanations because of W[ilfrid] having fatally insisted on sticking my name on the book of his travels.*—Anne Blunt, 1891[9]

Anne and Wilfrid Blunt, both English, trekked through the Syrian and Arabian deserts in 1877–78 and 1878–79. They undertook surveys, fleshing out inadequate maps; studied in detail the customs of the various Bedouin tribes; and learned Arabic, Anne becoming the more fluent of the two. The more time they spent with the dignified Bedouin, the less patience they had for their seemingly vulgar compatriots.

Anne also acquired pure Arab breeding stock and established a stud farm at Crabbet in England. Her matchmaking wasn't limited to horses: at Al Jawf, on their 1879 trek through the Nafud, she helped choose a bride for their guide, Mohammed ibn Aruk.

ABOVE: *Blunts' lodging at Ha'il, based on a watercolor by Anne Blunt.* G. Vuillier, artist. Blunt, *Tour du monde* 43: 1882, 40.

The Blunts made their way to the desert town of Ha'il, home to the Wahhabis, a fanatical sect of Islam, where they were hospitably received by the emir, Mohammed ibn Rashid, and where very few travelers had been before them. From there, they went to Baghdad, then to Persia. When they calculated that they had covered over 2,000 miles, the enormity of their accomplishment began to sink in.

FACING PAGE: *Lady Anne Blunt in Arab clothing.* Finch, *Wilfrid Scawen Blunt, 1840–1922,* facing p. 260.

This trip was especially difficult for Anne. An injured knee nearly cost her her life during an attack by Roala tribesmen; Wilfrid's horse, Ariel, was badly hurt in a capricious boar hunt; servants left them; and their increasingly ragged appearances lost them the respect they needed to proceed safely. The bottom hit when Wilfrid was struck with severe dysentery. Pushed to the depths of desperation, Anne converted to Catholicism after his recovery. Even so, she wrote of her adventures dispassionately, downplaying her courage and stoicism.

Anne, a somewhat enigmatic figure, denied writing her books about their Arabian travels, crediting Wilfrid, and she withstood years of his infidelities before leaving him in 1909. One of Wilfrid's devoted biographers, Edith Finch, admitted that Anne was an elusive subject but admired her keen mind and her diligence. "On the other hand," she wrote,

> [Anne] lacked the sympathy and imagination which often enabled
> [Wilfrid] to grasp the drift of words spoken in an almost unknown
> tongue and somehow convey his meaning in reply. She had less,
> much less of course, of the temperament of the artist . . . Her
> sketches and water-colours, though often charming are too metic-
> ulously correct to be of great interest. In fact Lady Anne was
> something of a pedant.[10]

Anne Blunt's self-effacement diminished her importance as a
partner in the couple's travels and as the influential travel writer
she deserves to be known as.

## BEYOND SCHOLARSHIP

*[Baghdad] is the real East, and it is stirring; things are happening
here, and the romance of it all touches me and absorbs me.*
—Gertrude Bell, 1914[11]

Where Dieulafoy, Edwards, and Blunt had distinguished themselves mainly through their learning, Gertrude Bell went far
beyond, becoming involved in the political transformation of
Mesopotamia during and after World War I.

Bell is an especially accessible traveler; through her many
books and copious letters, there was very little she did not com-
mit to paper, amorous relationships being exceptions. Born in
England in 1868, into a family of immense wealth, Bell was
given every advantage. Her life was charmed, idyllic, and comfortable, and, as biographer Elizabeth Burgoyne paraphrased
one of Bell's colleagues, "obstacles had a trick of melting away
when she encountered them." Bell graduated with a first in history from Lady Margaret Hall, one of only two colleges at
Oxford University open to women at that time.[12]

After several seasons of travel in Europe, Bell made her first
trip to the East in 1892, when she went overland to Persia with
Florence Lascelles, her cousin and the daughter of Sir Frank
Lascelles, Britain's ambassador to Iran. She began learning Farsi

and became briefly engaged to Henry Cadogan, a legation secretary. Her parents objected to Cadogan, and so, being a dutiful daughter, she returned to England. Cadogan accidentally drowned nine months later.

Bell's first book, *Safar Nameh: Persian Pictures,* 1894, was published anonymously. Her second, *Divan,* 1897, was a well-regarded translation of the work of the Persian poet Hafiz.

Travel became all-consuming. With friends or relatives, she roved Europe and North Africa and went around the world. She first visited Syria in November 1899, when she went to Jerusalem to see the Rosens, friends she had made in Teheran. With them, she toured Palestine and Transjordan, took up photography, and began studying Arabic. On her own, she traveled into Lebanon and to Palmyra.

She spent the next five years in Europe and on another round-the-world trip, with a brief visit to Palestine in 1902. She became an accomplished alpine climber and continued to study Farsi and Arabic.

Bell then embarked on the journey that resulted in *The Desert and the Sown* and launched her career as a Middle Eastern traveler. On 5 February 1905 she rode out of Jerusalem, accompanied by muleteers Muhammed, Ibrahim, and Habib, and Mikhail, a cook with a taste for alcohol in the form of arak. Her goal was Asia Minor, but her immediate destination was the Hauran region of southern Syria. The weather was discouragingly wet and cold, the terrain muddy and barren, but Bell's way was eased by desert hospitality; tents and houses were freely opened to her.

The idea of a woman occupied with archaeology was so

unusual that the Turkish vali, or governor, Nazim Pasha, became perturbed by reports of her trek. When she arrived in Damascus, she immediately arranged an audience with him to assure him that her pursuits were indeed archaeological.

Bell traveled on to Baalbek, then to Aleppo, where she hired Fattuh, a Syrian Christian, who was to be her guide for years to come. From there, she went to southern Turkey. As she traced inscriptions on Nabatean, Roman, and Greek monuments, her interest in archaeology grew. The many photographs she took began a collection that eventually numbered in the thousands.[13]

From February to August 1907, she was back in Turkey, this time working on inscriptions in churches with Sir William Ramsay, with whom she co-wrote *The Thousand and One Churches,* 1909. Also in 1907, she met Major Charles Doughty-Wylie of the Royal Welsh Fusiliers, the nephew of desert traveler Charles Doughty. He was married, but over the next seven years they fell in love and carried on an anguished correspondence, meeting only rarely, until his death at Gallipoli in 1915 during World War I.

In early 1909, Bell traveled to Mesopotamia to study Roman and Byzantine churches along the Euphrates River. She mapped the sites and made rubbings of Hittite inscriptions. Her next book, *Amurath to Amurath,* 1911, resulted from this trip. *Palace and Mosque at Ukhaidir,* 1914, incorporated material collected from subsequent trips.

In late 1913, Bell set out with Fattuh and a small crew of guides and porters through An Nafud to Ha'il, following the route taken by the Blunts. Her departure was not without obstacles: both the British and the Ottoman governments raised a fuss, then washed their hands of her. She carried basic survey equipment and took bearings with the hopes of filling in empty areas on the maps.

Arriving in Ha'il, the first European woman seen in the town since Anne Blunt, Bell wondered at the ease with which she got there, just as if she'd "been strolling along Piccadilly." Received by Ibrahim, the uncle of the emir, Sa'ud ibn Rashid, who was away, she was made an informal prisoner. Devious but polite means were used to keep her from departing: her camels were sent off to graze two days' journey away, and she could not leave without permission of the emir. Her attempt to draw much-needed money on her letter of credit was refused. She was eventually allowed to go, but she first insisted on being given a proper tour of the town. From Ha'il, she went to Baghdad, then to Damascus and Constantinople, returning home in May 1914.[14]

Bell began working in the war by tracking the missing and wounded in France, then transferred to British secret intelligence in Cairo and became part of the Mesopotamia Expeditionary Force in Basra and Baghdad. By Armistice Day in 1918, she was heavily involved in plans for what has variously been called Britain's mandate in, or treaty with, Iraq. In 1920, she became the Oriental secretary for Sir Percy Cox, the chief political officer of the British high commission for Mesopotamia. She worked well with Cox, but his temporary successor, A. T. Wilson, accused her of interfering in matters for which she was ill prepared and for being indiscreet in her correspondence. He tried but failed to have her removed.

Bell was instrumental in establishing Iraq's current borders, a rather contentious achievement from today's perspective. She was also involved in the appointment of Faisal as the first king of Iraq in 1921, an appointment that was ratified by a majority of Iraqi leaders chosen to represent the various tribes and regions. And, from 1923, she was Iraq's director of antiquities and founder of Baghdad's museum, now known as Iraq Museum International. She died just before her fifty-eighth birthday, in July 1926, from an overdose of sleeping pills and was buried in Baghdad. Whether her death was deliberate or accidental has never been determined.

A complex woman, Bell's independent spirit is unquestionable, yet she initially disapproved of female suffrage, and she sought and relied on her parents' opinions for many of her decisions. In 1913, she was one of the first women to be elected to the traditionally misogynist Royal Geographical Society★ and, in 1918, received the RGS Founder's Medal for Exploration. She was the third woman, after Lady Jane Franklin in 1860 and Mary Somerville in 1869, to receive such an award.[15]

By most accounts, Bell was well received by Arabs as a traveler, scholar, and political personage. King Faisal, during his early years in Iraq, depended on her extensive knowledge of the tribes and her good sense. Tribal leaders counted on her for guidance and information. Some men resented her, including Ibn Sa'ud, who was not accustomed to dealing with a woman on state affairs. He apparently assumed that Bell's involvement symbolized the British government's lack of respect for him.

Arabian explorer Wilfred Thesiger praised Bell's journey to Ha'il and considered her the only true female explorer of the Middle East. Yet Freya Stark, when asked to write a biography of Bell, admitted that she was not interested in the subject. Bell's ghost overshadowed Stark in Baghdad, where she settled for a brief time beginning in 1929. She thought Bell's accomplishments overrated but conceded that if the two had ever met, Bell probably would not have liked her very much either.[16]

Bell has been said to have condemned other women who presumed to stake a claim in the Middle East. Stark was apparently told by Violet Dickson of Kuwait that Bell's only comment when Violet's husband, British political agent Colonel Harold Dickson, introduced her to Bell, was, "It is such a pity you all marry and bring out incapable young wives." Rosita Forbes suffered much disparagement in Bell's letters. Bell accused her of "trumpet blowing," in response to Forbes's request to make a propaganda film for King Faisal, mocked her attempts to speak Arabic, and called her a "first-class busybody." Aside from Forbes, however, Bell's letters are filled with kind references to women and with disappointment that she had so few female friends.[17]

---

★In 1893, a small group, including Isabella Bird, had slipped in when the RGS briefly opened its doors to women. That door slammed shut soon after.

Vita Sackville-West, who stayed with her for a few days in Baghdad only months before Bell died, wrote, "She had the gift of making every one feel suddenly eager; of making you feel that life was full and rich and exciting." Bell had lived that full and rich life; it's only fair that she was able to pass some of the feeling along to others.[18]

Although Blunt, Dieulafoy, Edwards, and Bell are the best known, there were a number of women excavating in Egypt, surveying in Syria and Palestine, and studying documents at Mount Sinai, especially in the last years of the nineteenth century and after. It is difficult to pinpoint their inspirations for such careers, as records of their motivations are elusive. There is no doubt, however, that with the admittance of women into universities and the granting of degrees, it became easier for them to establish themselves as scholars, to become published, and to find funding for their projects.

## Bluestockings

*I swear the only thing that charms me is to speak without rhyme or reason about all that passes through my head, and I have not so much as entitled a chapter, when I sense myself taken by the desire to occupy myself with another subject.*—Olympe Audouard, 1866[19]

Olympe Audouard, the founder of two journals, *Le Papillon* and *La Revue cosmopolite,* was condemned by male contemporaries as a *bas-bleu,* or bluestocking. A late-eighteenth-century term that came to designate female intellectuals, it was used pejoratively by the mid-1800s. Both Audouard and writer Louise Colet, bluestockings as well as travelers to the East, were mercilessly attacked for their views.

Audouard's confessed fickleness of topic was only one of her many literary sins, the worst of which was feminism. Her outspoken advocacy of divorce—she had separated from her husband soon after marriage—earned her the label "bellicose." Her books on her stay in Egypt in 1864 and 1865, *Les Mystères de l'Égypte dévoilés, Les Mystères du sérail et des harems turcs,* and *L'Orient et ses peuplades,* do little to correct that impression, jumping, as they do, between objective reportage and irksome self-flattery. Audouard's writing highlighted the confusion of a woman who demanded freedom while taking offense at those who did not pay her homage. Unwilling to exercise discretion, she declared that Egypt's viceroy considered her a spy; then she justified his suspicions by criticizing the government at length.★ She had apparently decided that writing what she wished was part of her quest for freedom.[20]

Morality obsessed Audouard. About the women of the harem, she was of two minds. She saw the harem as a liberating space, yet she was disgusted by the intrigues she had heard of: male lovers entering the sacred confines wrapped in veils; women disguised as maids, slipping out to carry on adulterous affairs. In her books, she chose the most lurid stories and exaggerated their barbarity, emulating the seamier tales of the *Arabian Nights.*

As Jean-Marie Carré complained in his survey of the experiences of French travelers to Egypt: "Here a betrayed husband cuts the head off of an unfaithful spouse and has it carried in a bag to her lover. There an old pasha gives the order to suffocate . . . under the eyes of his guilty wives, the two children that they had from his rivals." In one especially horrific story, a pasha hacked a favorite but disobedient dancer into little pieces and had the bits transported in a lovely, flower-covered chest back to her friends. "Enough crimes and depravity, you say," Carré exclaimed. "Someone snatch the pen from this manufacturer of tittle-tattle!"[21]

For all of her moralizing, however, Audouard was captivated by the pure sensuality of the East. Of a night in the desert, she wrote, "From the garden came the soft fragrance of flowers, their

★Also associated with espionage was an earlier traveler of Dutch origins, Ida de Sainte-Elme (pseudonym for Elzelina Tolstoy van Aylde-Jonghe), author of *La Contemporaine en Égypte,* a collection of spurious and spicy gossip. A former courtesan, she had apparently been attached to Napoleon's secret police.

*Louise Colet.* Ivray, *L'Aventure Saint-Simonienne et les femmes,* 1928, facing p. 176.

sweet perfumes carried to me by a light breeze. This was the moment of the full moon . . . Never had nights appeared to me to be so splendidly beautiful; in face of this desert without end."[22]

Carré wasted no honeyed words on another Egyptian visitor, Louise Colet. A poet, essayist, epistolarian, and novelist, she was the former lover and muse of Gustave Flaubert and a key member of the Parisian literary world. She received numerous prizes for poetry from the Académie française and counted Victor Hugo, Alfred de Musset, and Alfred de Vigny among her friends yet was also condemned as a bluestocking. Her successes may have created jealousy among her acquaintances, including Alphonse Karr, whom she attempted to stab with a kitchen knife for his published insults about her affair with writer Victor Cousin, and author Maxime Du Camp, who disparaged her because of her affair with Flaubert.

Flaubert had broken with Colet before he and Du Camp went to Egypt in 1849. They reunited on his return but parted finally and acrimoniously in 1854. Before this split, she was incensed to read in his notes a detailed description of his sexual encounters with Kuchuk Hanem, a dancer in Esna, a town on the Nile in Upper Egypt. He assured her that the dancer felt nothing for him either emotionally or physically; she liked him only because he paid her. But Colet's concerns highlighted for him the differences between men and women. "Decidedly they are not the same, no matter what people say," he concluded.[23]

When she was nearly sixty, Colet went to Egypt to cover the inauguration of the Suez Canal for *Le Siècle*. She was the only woman with such an assignment; the others present, like the Duchesse de Persigny, were in Empress Eugénie's suite or were invitees of Ferdinand de Lesseps.

The male writers on the junket shunned or mocked Colet for her faded beauty and her anti-imperialism. She was accorded few of the honors she felt she deserved; in Cairo, she was lodged at the Europe, the lowest-quality hotel of those booked for the Suez delegation. For the trip up the Nile, the best of the viceroy's steamers was for select visitors; Colet was on the *Gizeh,* a rubbish heap filled with cockroaches, mosquitoes, and foul latrine odors. The squalid conditions drove her to double her usual nightly doses of opium.[24]

Colet may have intended to thoroughly tour the monuments, but the heat and her poor health sapped her energy. The ghost of her former lover haunted her, but of Esna she mentioned only the high temperature and her rush through the bazaar.

She submitted two articles, one under the pseudonym Mohammed el-Akmar, and her unfinished *Les Pays lumineux* was published posthumously. "A tasty psychological document," wrote Carré, "this is no longer the 'turbulent, curse-calling, frothing Muse' . . . but still the mannered, lyrical and insupportable woman, who draws all to her, who calls us to witness the injustices of her lot and her world, speaks with us of her illnesses and vapours."[25]

Colet and Audouard were dismissed as self-absorbed and demanding. They trespassed on male territory, but worse still, they never apologized.

## WORKING WIVES
Isabel Burton (1831–96) & Regula Engel (1761–1853)

*One can see very well, Madame, that you are an Englishwoman. A Frenchwoman would have at least fainted or have been taken by a fit of hysterics, and you are so calm and practical, that one would say you are classifying baubles instead of human bones, and I swear that this disgusts me, that I wish you had a bit more sensitivity.*
—Count Perrochel to Isabel Burton, 1875[26]

It was with great satisfaction that Isabel Burton reported this pronouncement by Count Perrochel on her zest for work at Palmyra. She was there exploring with her husband, Richard, and was of the opinion that if she were the sort that fell into "shrieking convulsions," she would be not only a burden but a bore.[27]

Like other women with an occupation, Isabel Burton believed that travel alone was not enough; time had to be filled meaningfully. All women were destined to carry out duties; those of the traveling wife were to

ABOVE: *The Burtons' house in Salihiyya, at that time a village, now a quarter in Damascus.* Frederic Leighton, artist. Burton, The Inner Life of Syria, 1879 [1875], facing p. 80.

FACING PAGE: *Isabel Burton.* Burton, The Inner Life of Syria, 1879 [1875], frontispiece.

ride well, walk, swim, shoot, and learn to defend herself if attacked, so as not to be entirely dependent upon the husband; also to make the bed, arrange the tent, cook the dinner if necessary, wash the clothes by the river side, mend and spread them to dry—for his comfort; nurse the sick, bind and dress wounds, pick up a language, make a camp of natives love, respect, and obey her; groom her own horse, saddle him, learn to wade him through rivers; sleep on the ground with the saddle for a pillow, and generally learn to rough it, and do without comforts. She must be thoroughly useful to her husband, and try never to want anything of him. She ought to be able to write, and to help him in taking his observations; and if she can sketch or paint, she is indeed a happy woman.[28]

*"Our Desert Camp."*
Charles Tyrwhitt-Drake, artist. Burton,
*The Inner Life of Syria,* 1879 [1875],
facing p. 172.

Because Richard was demanding and unpredictable, Isabel's job was to stay one step ahead of him in planning, at his side in companionship, and one step behind him in deference. She confessed that if she had been born a man, she would have wanted to be Richard Burton. Being a woman, she settled for being his wife.

Isabel not only emulated Richard but also had heroines; she proclaimed her desire to become the fifth of a "small knot of ladies . . . Lady Mary Wortley Montagu, Lady Hester Stanhope, Lady Ellenborough [Jane Digby], and the Princesse de la Tour d'Auvergne."★[29]

★The Princesse de la Tour d'Auvergne funded the building of the church of Jerusalem's present-day "Carmel of the Pater," in 1856. Burton pointed out that the princess was called eccentric because, like Digby and Stanhope, she had "wearied of the flesh-pots of Europe."[30]

In 1798, Zurich-born Regula Engel reluctantly put seven of her eight children in the care of friends and followed her much-loved husband, Colonel Florian Engel, to Egypt, where he was to fight with Napoleon. Indeed, Florian was surprised she would hesitate, declaring that only death would part them. Permission was granted for her and thirteen other women—one Swiss, the others French—to join the troops, on condition they weren't pregnant. Regula, who also took her youngest child out with her, bore twins shortly after their arrival in Cairo.

*Jaffa, the scene of Napoleon's Syrian campaign of 1799.*
J.J. Crew, artist; J.D. Woodward, engraver.
Wilson, *Picturesque Palestine*, 1881, vol. 2, facing p. 142.

Her brief account of this portion of her exciting life chronicled Napoleon's attack on Alexandria, the long trek to Cairo and her giving birth to another set of twins there, violent uprisings in Cairo against the French, and the march to Syria. At Jaffa she donned an officer's uniform and helped command a post. She wrote that her "martial attitude," along with her shapely Swiss calves, enhanced by the tight trousers of her stylish lieutenant's garb, won her much admiration.[31]

However, the French were defeated, many lost to disease and malnutrition, and they made their way back to Egypt, then France. Landing in Nice, Regula realized she was pregnant again. She bore twenty-one children in all, ten of whom died in battles, including Marengo and Waterloo. Her husband also died at Waterloo.

*I think no women have so much liberty . . . as the Turkish—and I think them, in their manner of living, capable of being the happiest creatures breathing.*—Lady Elizabeth Craven, 1789

# The Liberating Veil
## HAREMS & EASTERN WOMEN

FOR THE NINETEENTH-CENTURY WESTERN WOMAN, a visit to a harem, the secluded women of a Muslim family, was de rigueur, as it was one of the few things that she could do that her countrymen could not. Better yet, unlike other activities limited to women, harem visits were something men wanted to hear about. Firsthand knowledge gave travelers authority; thus, harems became a dominant motif in many women's accounts.

Readers and reviewers eagerly anticipated all details, especially those confirming their beliefs that harems were hotbeds of vice. But society disapproved of overt mention of sex, parts of the body, even undergarments, so such references had to be couched in innuendo to obscure them to all but the most astute reader.★

Harems, in the popular view of the West, were replicas of the most famous of all, that of Sultan Süleyman the Magnificent, established in 1541 in the Grand Seraglio at Constantinople's Topkapi Palace. It was headed by Süleyman's sultana, his former concubine, Hurrem Sultan, a Circassian whose fame spread to the West under the name of Roxelana. Traditionally, sultans did

★Certain male authors—Richard Burton, for example—rendered delicate passages of their books in Latin for the benefit of learned men (and, inadvertently, learned women).

"The Jewel of the Harem." Leopold Carl Müller, artist.
Ebers, *L'Égypte*, vol. 1, 1883, 59.

not marry; Hurrem/Roxelana somehow convinced Süleyman that it was time for a change. Not only did she rule the harem with an iron fist, reputedly talking Süleyman into murdering his first son to make way for hers, but her name was immortalized in dozens of plays and tales by the likes of Jean Racine, Charles-Louis de Secondat Montesquieu, and Jean-François Marmontel. Large harems, such as Süleyman's, consisting of multiple wives, concubines, female relatives, children, and slaves, ostensibly existed until the early twentieth century.[1]

The word "harem," which derives from the Arabic *haram,* means, among other things, protected, forbidden, and sanctuary, and refers to either the women or the place of seclusion. Islam allows any man rich enough to provide for his wives to marry up to four, but a harem can also be a single wife. Muslim women had varying degrees of freedom, from absolute confinement, in high-status families, to relative liberty, in rural areas and among the lower classes.[2]

Visitors to harems can be divided into those who sought similarities to their own lives and those who sought differences. The former focused on such details as familiar customs or articles of clothing; the latter emphasized the more exotic features of smoking a chibouque (a long-stemmed pipe) or a nargileh (a water pipe) and eating with fingers. Some were fascinated by the material trappings—clothing, cosmetics, and décor, especially— others were intent on learning something of attitudes and talents. All were influenced by expectations, and either group could experience a delightful visit or a vexatious and boring one.

Overall, it is difficult to come to any broad conclusions about Western women's prejudices or preconceptions about harems. It is even harder to determine how Eastern women viewed their visitors, as most of their responses available today have been filtered back to us through Westerners. What is evident, however, is that the factors determining how the women saw each other were as variable as the women themselves.

Many women, like Lady Mary Wortley Montagu, believed that harems were embodiments of the *Arabian Nights* and confessed to craving such an experience. As the nineteenth century progressed, however, others, including Princess Cristina di Belgiojoso, tried their best to obliterate this myth:

> We've been told that these places are the abodes of beauty and of love: we are led to believe that the written descriptions, even if exaggerated and embellished, are, however, founded on reality and that it is in these mysterious retreats that one can find assembled all the marvels of luxury, art, magnificence and voluptuousness. How far we are from the truth![3]

## THE HAREM SYSTEM

*The fact of the harem surprises me still. I open my eyes, I see, and I still doubt.*—Valérie de Gasparin, 1866[4]

The progressive woman was prepared to be more or less shocked by the mere existence of harems, having informed herself with countless Oriental tales of dubious reliability. But much of her attitude depended on her place in society.

*Harem scene.* Mary Walker, artist.
Hornby, *Constantinople,* 1863,
facing p. 321.

Many descriptions were written by upper-class women, including the unshockable Lady Montagu. In her enduring portrayals of elite harems and *hammams,* or baths, she strove to counter previous accounts, all by men, who could not have had firsthand knowledge. She argued that the harem was not the fleshpot envisioned by Europeans. Rather, it was a society of women for themselves, complete and secure, and independent of male control. The women regulated who they would see and when, even their husbands. Their clothing, far from hampering freedom, ensured it, as they could go about in public without revealing their identities. Montagu's defense of what seemed to be a backward practice, especially for someone as forward thinking as she, was revolutionary.★

No less original were her candid depictions of scantily clad women (by European standards) comfortably lounging

★Montagu put envy into action when she left her husband in 1739, and she lived on the Continent until after his death in 1761.

together, as any suggestion of intimacy, even if innocent of sexuality, was one of many forbidden topics. However, she failed to make them acceptable for women to either write of or read of, as society sanctimoniously judged her imprudent. All the same, visitors to harems could suggest certain unmentionable scenes by simply invoking her name in their own written accounts, while deflecting criticism of themselves.

Lady Elizabeth Craven, at Constantinople in 1786, affirmed the notion of freedom by praising the robes and veils that protected women from the gaze of strangers. On other points, including beauty and fashion, however, she contradicted Montagu.★[5]

Julia Pardoe also believed in Eastern women's inherent liberty. Concluding her description of the delightful atmosphere of the harem in her *Beauties of the Bosphorus*, she wrote, "All this may, and indeed must appear startling, to persons who have accustomed themselves to believe that Turkish wives were morally manacled slaves. There are, probably, no women so little trammelled in the world; so free to come and to go unquestioned." She found it laughable that ignorant Westerners should be so firmly convinced that harems were immoral.[6]

Montagu, Craven, and Pardoe emphasized how all women in the harem, whether wife, concubine, or slave, coexisted as if equals—rivalry aside—but they avoided the subject of polygamy. In the 1840s, however, socially conscious middle-class women started to travel. Polygamy became their focus, even though they were too reserved to openly state their belief that it was a form of sexual exploitation. Harriet Martineau, an outspoken abolitionist who supported herself by writing about social issues, couched her criticisms in terms of slavery. Her brief visits to two harems, one in Cairo, the other in Damascus, led her to declare, "If we are to look for a hell upon earth, it is where polygamy exists." Harems saddened her more than even

---

★Craven accused the mischievous Horace Walpole of penning Montagu's letters. She declared she could "feel the scratches of the cloven claw of a male scholar in every line."[7]

"Deaf and Dumb schools, Lunatic Asylums, or even Prisons."[8]

Martineau had been warned to lay her prejudices aside and was subsequently censured for her pronouncements, but she claimed that she had earnestly tried to understand the harem system. "I always before believed that every arrangement and prevalent practice had some one fair side, some one redeeming quality: and diligently did I look for this fair side in regard to polygamy: but there is none. The longer one studies the subject, and the deeper one penetrates into it,—the more is one's mind confounded with the intricacy of its iniquity."[9]

Feminist Olympe Audouard, wielding a pen far more daring than most women of her time, tackled such taboos as divorce and sexuality. Sojourns in the East in the mid-1860s supplied her with enough material to fill three books, yet she remained ambiguous about her specific objections to polygamy, resorting to spicily inaccurate innuendo, vague wording, or frequent insertions of the notorious dashes and ellipsis points.

It seems that Audouard was torn in her opinions about harems. She criticized them but, like Montagu, also admired them as female domains, where women could be themselves, away from the influence of men. For this reason, the veil, too, drew her praise. This virtue, however, did not overcome the shamefulness of immorality, ignorance, and servility. She disparaged Egyptian women's indecent conversations about love, believing that such talk was as damaging to the young as blatantly licentious behavior. Egyptian girls might rigorously protect their physical virginity, she observed, but "one thing they don't have, and it's even unknown with them, and that's moral virginity."[10]

*Emmeline Lott.* Lott, The "English governess" in Egypt, [1866], frontispiece.

Audouard's books came out around the same time as Emmeline Lott's The *"English Governess" in Egypt.* Lott was a self-proclaimed former companion to the harem of Egyptian viceroy Ismail Pasha and governess to his six-year-old son, the "Grand Pacha."* Lucie Duff Gordon wrote that the few harems she knew were unlike those described by Lott and added that Lott's and Audouard's books were examples of "odious" Cairo gossip.[11]

Cristina di Belgiojoso visited many harems in Turkey and Syria in 1852, but instead of the gorgeous, tapestried palaces seen by Montagu and Craven or the dens of iniquity reported on by Audouard, Belgiojoso encountered dirt, poverty, undisciplined children, women in tatters, idleness, and spiritual barrenness. Immorality and degradation she took for granted

---

*Lott is often mentioned in books about harems and women travelers, but I have yet to find any biographical material on her. Her harem accounts are repetitive and lack convincing detail. Much of The *"English Governess"* is consumed with petty grievances against the German factotums of Ismail Pasha, as well as against the German maids employed in the harem. Venom not expended upon these persons was directed against the women of the harem, their slaves, and the viceroy.

*"The Flute Player (Harem Interior; Constantinople, 1860),"* by French artist Henriette Browne. Browne traveled to Constantinople and North Africa and painted a number of canvases with Eastern themes. Jérusalémy, Tour du monde 8: 1863, 145.

because of the polygamy. She especially believed that harems pandered to female frailty and encouraged foolishness:

> To be angry without reason, to not have common-sense, to speak in error and at cross purposes, to do the opposite that one asks of you and above all that one orders you to do, to not work unless it pleases, to spend money earned by the husband extravagantly, to claim illness and to complain without rhyme or reason, those are her privileges.[12]

Belgiojoso came to expect ignorance and, during a visit in the Turkish town of Payas, was warned by Mustuk Bey that his wife was incapable of intelligent conversation. Belgiojoso, however, was pleased when Mme Mustuk

> took off her mask of fierce timidity and chatted for some time with perfect ease. She asked me many questions about our customs . . . My lovely hostess wasn't as limited as her husband deigned to believe, in seeing the interest that she took about a multitude of things that didn't have anything to do with her, and the perseverance with which she asked me *why* over everything.[13]

Most visitors were impatient with the idleness. Amelia Edwards met women in a village north of Luxor who were "absolutely without mental resources; and they were even without the means of taking air and exercise. One could see that time hung heavy on their hands, and that they took but a feeble interest in the things around them." To Edwards, the impoverished fellahin, farmers laboring in the open air, were far happier. Jane Digby, who spent much time in harems, expressed no definitive opinion. Of Abd al-Qadir's harem, she deplored the women's wasted lives; of others, she told a visitor that she delighted in their "simple but genuine employments." The women's earthy conversations, however, never ceased to disturb her.[14]

Some visitors went so far as to question whether Eastern women were of the same species. German traveler Countess Ida von Hahn-Hahn wrote that the women of the harem she visited in the early 1840s were dull-witted, and that "a woman without intelligence is no longer a woman, but, alas! . . . she becomes simply *une femelle.*" Audouard used almost the same words in describing certain Egyptian women: *Ce sont des femelles, et non des femmes,* "They are females, not women." Harriet Martineau, on visiting baths in Palestine, wrote that the bathers' loud chatter sent her and her companion, Mrs Yates, rushing outside "stunned and breathless. To this moment, I find it difficult to think of these creatures as human beings."[15]

Lucie Duff Gordon did not visit many harems, high-class or otherwise, but she did live among Egyptians and believed that she was better acquainted with them than many long-term European residents. She wrote often of her meetings with Egyptian women in her characteristic terms of humanity and tolerance. She was not alone in feeling amity for these women: Hester Stanhope expressed warmth toward the widow of Mourad Bey, whom she visited in Cairo: "[She] is the most charming woman . . . I ever knew, the picture of a captive queen, with extraordinary talents, the tenderest heart, and the most affectionate manner. I should like to return to Cairo, if it was only to see this woman, for whom I have a real friendship and admiration."[16]

Both Duff Gordon and Stanhope managed to communicate with the women despite the lack of a common language, and both eventually learned Arabic. But most visitors wrote of the struggle to be understood and the boredom of sitting around with little to say and no way to say it. When Harriet Martineau's female interpreter did not show up for her visit, she and Mrs Yates were obliged to fend for themselves. For Martineau, sign language was of no help between people of such different cultures. Martineau was also almost completely deaf and found conversation, even in English, trying.[17]

Long pauses gave Western women a chance to form vivid, if not always accurate, pictures of their hostesses and their surroundings. All too often, a single two- or three-hour visit drew criticism of unwonted sensuality, manifested in endless bathing, grooming, lounging, smoking, and caressing. The visits also provoked the ever-popular disapproval of insalubriousness. For fastidious Victorian women, especially, this reported aspect of harem life was the chief aggravation. The main delights were comradeship, the apparent love of children, and displays of beauty and finery.

## FASHION IN THE HAREM

*I am* femmelette *enough to have taken particular notice of the dress, which, if female envy did not spoil every thing in the world of women, would be graceful.*—Lady Elizabeth Craven, 1789[18]

ABOVE: *"A Veiled Beauty."* Drawing by F. C. Welsch. Ebers, *L'Égypte,* vol. 1, 1883, 88.
FACING PAGE: *Turkish woman in a* yashmak *(veil) and* feradge *(cloak), c. 1890.* Unidentified photographer.

Critiques of fashion and beauty made up the largest part of the harem account by far. Any comments, however, are suspect when one realizes how judgmental women travelers of all nationalities were of other women. German women thought English women aged poorly; English women

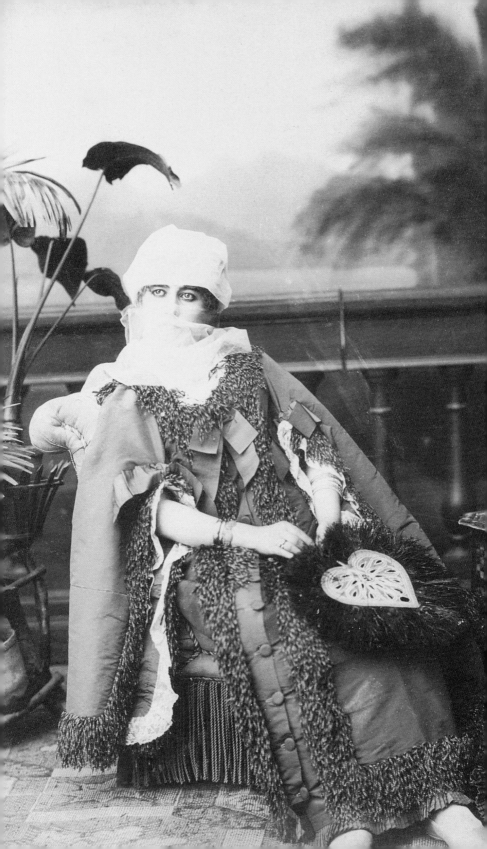

*Lady Mary Wortley Montagu at a Turkish bath.* Daniel Chodowiecki, artist. Montagu, *Letters of the Right Honourable Lady M-y W-y M-e*, Berlin, 1781, frontispiece. Courtesy of Department of Special Collections, Charles E. Young Research Library, UCLA.

accused Italian women of the same weakness; French women believed only they knew how to dress well. Most agreed that Eastern women were beautiful in their bloom but that idleness and the heavy use of cosmetics ravaged their faces early.

Lady Montagu set the tone when she admired the lovely complexions and fine heads of hair and approved of the plucked eyebrows. She was intrigued by the application of kohl around the eyes, though she believed it too startling for Englishwomen to adopt. She thought less of the habit of tinting the fingernails pink. Clothing and adornments, especially jewelry, also drew her praise. But sometimes there were no clothes to describe. She shocked her readers by declaring that the Turkish women she met in the baths were "in the state of nature, that is, in plain English, stark naked, without any beauty or defect concealed."[19]

Thirty-six-year-old Elizabeth Craven was of the opinion that "hot-baths destroy the solids, and these women at nineteen look older than I am at this moment. They endeavour to repair by art the mischief their constant soaking does to their charms."[20]

When Ida von Hahn-Hahn met the sister and wife of Egyptian minister Rifat Pasha, she described their pleasant

manners and hospitality, then sharpened her pencil and declared she could not find "the slightest trace of beauty in any one of them." The pasha's sister's face was "too fat and globular, and her figure generally is so rotund that she constantly gives you an idea of a large full moon." Hahn-Hahn complimented the purple jacket and the silk gown with

*Emilia Hornby in her house in Therapia, north of Constantinople and overlooking the Bosporus.* Mary Walker, artist. Hornby, *Constantinople,* 1863, facing p. 38.

slits up the sides with the qualification that "both articles of dress fitted so tightly to the body that it was really wonderful how the body's fulness could be kept within those bounds."[21]

Englishwoman Emilia Hornby, in Constantinople during the Crimean War, was a frequent guest at rich harems and received Turkish women in her home. She enthused over their alluring *yashmaks* and cloaks of vibrant purples and greens. Of those who gathered at the local rendezvous, the Valley of the Sweet Waters, she wrote: "Nothing . . . could be more strikingly beautiful than these clusters of women by the trees and fountain. Imagine five or six in a row; their jet-black eyes shining through their white veils, under which you can see the gleam of jewels which confine their hair."[22]

She further praised the young, who were "*cultivated* to the highest perfection of physical beauty ... their skin is literally as white as their veils, with the faintest tinge of pink on the cheek, like that in the inside of a shell." But she could not resist adding that age set in quickly, "the skin becomes yellow and sickly-looking, and you long to give the yashmak a pull and admit a fresh breeze to brighten up the fine features."[23]

Eastern women were also fascinated by Western women's clothing. Bathers in Sophia in 1717 were amazed at Montagu's stays, thinking that they were some kind of "machine" devised by her husband. Lady Mary Elgin's beaded and spangled court gown was admired by the sultan's mother, the valide sultana, in 1801, in a manner that reminded Elgin of Montagu's descriptions. For her part, Elgin noted that although the valide did not display many diamonds, what she did have on were "thumpers." She marveled at how the woman tucked her legs up under her as she relaxed on her sofa.[24]

By midcentury, with fashionable women such as Hornby living in Constantinople, the European styles caught on. Turkish women studied their visitors' attire as closely as they studied the latest Paris magazines, and couturiers opened shops for their convenience. They replaced their trousers, caftans, and vests with low-cut gowns, burdened with bustles and hoops. Emily Beaufort believed that the immodest 1860s fashions would have "scandalized" Montagu.[25]

By the 1870s, European dress was worn as a matter of course in loftier circles. Round-the-world traveler Lady Annie Brassey described Mme Hilmeh Bey, the daughter of Fuad Pasha: "[She] received us in a French *robe de matinée,* a blue cashmere beautifully embroidered with wreaths of roses, *crêpe lisse* ruffs and frills, a pile of dyed golden hair (naturally black) rolled and twisted and curled in the latest fashion."[26]

## Emancipated Harems

*The women of the higher classes . . . all bemoan their present hard fate very much. It is a great mistake of the Turks to think they can educate their wives and daughters, and still keep them in confinement of subjection.*—Lady Annie Brassey, 1880[27]

As the nineteenth century progressed, more women wrote of the need for emancipation in harems and commented on the growing number of harem women who aspired to what Europeans considered a broader and more meaningful life.

Emily Beaufort was encouraged to hear that upper-class harems, at least, were changing. She noted that women "read French and play on the pianoforte, besides occupying themselves with many kinds of embroidery, and some even sing and draw: One Pasha's wife was mentioned to us who had lately played the whole of the 'Trovatore' by heart." She was concerned, however, that these skills were being imparted by "French governesses and *femmes de chambre,*" altogether undesirable groups, in her opinion, from which to draw teachers. "Formerly," Beaufort observed, "if they had not intelligence enough to be useful and good, they were at least in happy ignorance of many of the vices to which they are now addicted." She concluded that visits from European women were harmful, "for when they see us going and coming and rejoicing in our own liberty, they fancy that we must use that liberty for only the same objects as they would."[28]

On a trip to Constantinople in 1878, Annie Brassey was astonished at the many advances that had been made since her visit four years earlier. She heard that Princess Nazli, the progressive granddaughter of viceroy Muhammad 'Ali, had gone to Egypt but had been forbidden to leave. With some borrowed money, however, the princess and her English maid veiled themselves and slipped away. Once out of sight of Cairo, they "threw off yashmak and feridjee and travelled as two English ladies, until they reached Constantinople, when they again assumed the

"*Egyptian Women,*"
*sketched by artist*
*Elizabeth Butler during*
*her stay in Egypt in 1885.*
*Butler was well known for*
*her accurate and detailed*
*paintings of military*
*subjects.* Butler, From Sketch-book
and Diary, 1909, 28.

Oriental costume." Brassey noted that a few years earlier, the women would have been stuffed into a sack and thrown into the Bosporus for their behavior, referring to a former method of disposing of no-longer-desired wives and concubines.[29]

Relatively few Western women had opportunities, or took advantage of those few they had, to meet Eastern women outside the formal harem setting. Aside from Lucie Duff Gordon, there was Sarah Belzoni, who lived among women in Luxor and Aswan off and on from around 1815 to 1818. She described her acquaintances and her struggles to communicate with them, having little knowledge of Arabic. For her, visits with Egyptian women were painful: she was tormented by their curiosity but admitted that they treated her with kindness. Her experience was made worse when she became totally, though temporarily, blind from ophthalmia while living in a room in Karnak with six other women. Sarah had gone to Egypt with her husband, Giovanni. His preoccupation with antiquities and his frequent absences while excavating in Abu Simbel and Thebes meant that she was on her own for much of the time. Her brief and rather sorrowful account may have been the result of her loneliness rather than her inability to adapt.[30]

Valérie de Gasparin, a Swiss Calvinist who traveled through Egypt and Syria with her husband in 1848, made a concerted effort to meet ordinary women, as she was determined to improve their lot through Christianity. Everywhere the couple went they distributed sewing supplies and religious tracts. In Assiut, she met a group of fellahin, whom she pitied because of their poverty and ignorance, and seriously considered buying one and converting her.[31]

## The View from the Harem

*They envy us our knowledge and independence, and they deplore the*
*way they are kept, and their not being able to know or do anything.*
—Isabel Burton, 1875[32]

Western women frequently mentioned what they believed
Eastern women thought of them, though there is scant firsthand evidence to back them up. One charming and credible
account comes from Annie Brassey, who had been openly
admiring a young woman in Constantine, Algeria, in 1880. The
woman told Brassey, "You like to look at us, we like to look at
you. You're quite as strange to us as we are to you." Brassey
recounted their conversation, during "which she and her friends
evinced the greatest interest in knowing exactly what we had
been doing and where we had been going."[33]

Princess Maria Theresa Asmar of Mesopotamia, a rare
Eastern travel writer, wrote in her *Memoirs of a Babylon Princess*,
1844, of meeting Hester Stanhope in Lebanon, while a companion of the wife of Emir Beshir. She was startled to discover
that this tall figure in masculine dress was a woman. The two
had numerous conversations, Stanhope discoursing on the stars
and Asmar trying, but ever failing, to talk of her proposed travels in Europe and her hopes to witness "Christian virtues."
Stanhope disparaged European Christianity and urged her to
stay put.[34]

The idea of travel, it appeared, was incomprehensible to
most Eastern women, few of whom ventured out of their
homes. When told that Valérie de Gasparin had crossed Greece
on horseback, a Cairene woman reportedly sighed, "European
women are like men!" On another occasion, after admitting she
was childless, Gasparin spoke of going to Jerusalem. Her host-
ess asked if she was going there to pray for children. (The
modern-day woman traveler to the Middle East will be familiar with some variation of this question.) The youngest
daughter of the viceroy warned Gasparin that she would waste

*A Persian woman of Kashan. Woodcut from photo by Jane Dieulafoy.* Dieulafoy, *Tour du monde* 46: 1883, 111.

away if she went by camel to Syria. The women were convinced that her husband forced her to follow him, and they pitied her.[35]

Two Persian women waiting to be photographed by Jane Dieulafoy took advantage of Jane's preoccupation with her camera to discuss Farangui women: "In Farangistan . . . women are much unhappier than us. Their men make them work." From these and many other examples, it appears that Eastern women did not envy Western women's careers.[36]

As education advanced and opportunities expanded, one gets the sense that Eastern women grew tired of being put on view. American Anna Bowman Dodd, visiting Constantinople in 1902, was told that the sultan had banned foreigners from his harem and the ladies, it was rumored, preferred it that way. This was one woman's reason:

Why, after all, should we be expected to receive American or English ladies who are entirely unknown to us? We no longer wear the old dress. We dress as they do, only our gowns are more splendid. They wear muslins, even in public. Who of us would go abroad with so poor a gown? If they come to pay us a visit, it is that they may see us, look upon us, scrutinise us as they would actresses in a play. Why should we be willing to put on a dress we have discarded, and go into our old-fashioned Turkish rooms, to play the play they have come to see? . . . I dress as these ladies dress; I smoke cigarettes, as they smoke them; my rooms are as exact a copy of theirs as I can make them.[37]

## The Twentieth Century

*The* habara *and veil are not part of our religion, you know. They will have to be done away with very soon, in a few years, perhaps a few months, not for themselves, but of what they represent. But they are very becoming and women will hate to part with them.*—Mme Saad Zaghlul Pasha, quoted by Grace Thompson Seton, 1923[38]

By 1900, the East was in the midst of rapid change. The initial waves of explorers, merchants, diplomats, and independent travelers had given way to organized batches of tourists traveling with companies like Cook's, largely sequestered from contact with local people.

*Mme Saad Zaghlul Pasha, one of the politically active Egyptian women interviewed by Grace Thompson Seton in 1919. Seton, A Woman Tenderfoot in Egypt, 1923, facing p. 20.*

In Egypt, Britain was starting its third decade of its occupation. British bureaucrats and clerks arrived with their wives, who socialized with each other rather than with Egyptian women. In this aloof expatriate community, British women were neither open-minded nor interested. French and Italian women, plentiful in Egypt earlier, were now rare.

In Iraq, Gertrude Bell believed that British wives "take no interest in what's going on, know no Arabic and see no Arabs. They create an exclusive (it's also very second rate) English society quite cut off from the life of the town." Freya Stark's attempt to live in an Iraqi home in Baghdad created a scandal among expatriates.[39]

*A modern Egyptian family: the Keladas of Cairo, late 1920s.*

With the dispersal of the Turkish sultan's harem in 1909, harem visits, such as they had been described, became a thing of the past, though the harem—in the broader sense of the word, as a place of women—continues to exist. In accounts written by Western women, Eastern women, especially Egyptian, Turkish, and Syrian, became more clearly defined as individuals.

Rosita Forbes, traveling in the 1920s, vividly described her Syrian acquaintances, who had been fighting simultaneously for the freedom of their country— first against the Turks, then against the French—and for themselves. Forbes admired their sense of proportion, a result of this dual battle for liberty. She asked her friend Zarifa how she could bear her upcoming arranged marriage to an older man. "What a lot of importance you attach to men," was her friend's reply. To another friend, Forbes promoted the "ideal married life. I spoke of love, comradeship, and mutual interests, of doing everything together, of how an English husband expected his wife to golf with him and hunt with him, to share his play as well as his work." Her friend was appalled and asked if all "European husbands [were] as trying as that."[40]

American Grace Thompson Seton was one of several travelers who went to the East specifically to report on the progress of women's emancipation there. Her book *A Woman Tenderfoot in Egypt* surveyed the beginnings of Egyptian women's emancipation in 1911 and introduced to the West members of "The

Ladies' Delegation of Independence," formed in 1919. She admitted that the idea that a former occupant of a harem would work publicly to improve social conditions might surprise some readers. But it was an undeniable phenomenon, attributable, in part, to World War 1, the rise of feminism elsewhere, and prosperity brought by stability and increased trade. Especially active were the wives of banished political agitators, who had remained in the country to carry on their husbands' work.

The harem had been a mirror by which Western women could assess and assert their own independence. Eighteenth- and early-nineteenth-century travelers, believing that harem women had lives free of cares and that they could go about at will, veiled against unwanted attention, thought of the harem as a role model for freedom. From the 1840s on, travelers tended to suggest that harem women were enslaved. They compared their own ability to travel freely and their own occupations and found them worthier than those of harem women. Because the harem, as they saw it, no longer exists, we must rely to a certain extent on these pronouncements. They leave us no closer to an overall cohesive portrait, but they most emphatically attacked that fantasy still held today—that the harem was the mythic embodiment of Oriental splendor.

In both centuries, the Western woman's unique position within her society as an observer of harems meant that she was free to write about their superficial aspects, especially fashion and domesticity. At the same time, current moral standards dictated restraint in giving opinions about love and sexuality; frankness, even when obscured by allusion, drew criticism. That women were able to publish accounts of their travels was significant in itself.

# A HAREM ADVOCATE
## Lady Mary Wortley Montagu (1689–1762)

Lady Mary Wortley Montagu's fame resulted from her travels to Constantinople with her husband, British ambassador Edward Montagu, who had been sent there in 1716 to negotiate peace between the sultan and Europe. Lady Mary had no aspirations to help Edward with his duties. Perhaps she should have, as his efforts were deemed unsatisfactory and he was recalled early. The notable absence of Edward's diplomatic activities in her letters (in fact, his almost complete absence) suggests that she realized his impact on the Turks would be inadequate. She may have resolved to make up for this by becoming a one-woman delegation responsible for opening the West's eyes to the justness and

*Lady Mary Wortley Montagu with her son, Edward, and attendants. Attributed to Jean Baptiste Vanmour, c. 1717.* Courtesy The National Portrait Gallery, London (3924).

goodness of the East, a region she considered woefully and unfairly misrepresented. That she consorted only with elite Turkish society did not prevent her from making general pronouncements on the state of their empire and on the liberty of their women.

Modeling herself after the Eastern women she so admired, Lady Mary posed in Turkish attire for her portrait in 1717, possibly the first European woman to do so. Soon after, upperclass European women who had never so much as considered traveling to Constantinople were sporting flattering turbans, sashes, and slippers and had their portraits painted by such Orientalist artists as Jean-Étienne Liotard, who depicted, among others, Héléne Glavani, Maria Adelaide de Francia, and Maria Gunning, Countess of Coventry, in Turkish dress. Thanks, in part, to Lady Mary, harem style—the clothing of women who, in Lady Mary's words, "[were] more free than any ladies in the universe"—had made its way West.[41]

Lady Mary's descriptions of her visits to harems and baths in Sophia, Adrianople, and Constantinople were written up in unconventionally indiscreet letters. They went into private circulation in 1724 but were first published in 1763 as *Letters of the Right Honourable Lady M--y W---y M---e; Written During her Travels in Europe, Asia, and Africa, to Persons of Distinction, Men of Letters, &c. in Different Parts of Europe*. Her Turkish embassy letters and others written from the Continent have since been continuously reprinted or reissued in new editions. Lady Mary has been the subject of at least six biographies and has been included in most travel anthologies and studies.

# ARBITERS *of* FASHION
## Lady Elizabeth Craven (1750–1828) &
## Countess Ida von Hahn-Hahn (1805–80)

The adulterous and wealthy Lady Elizabeth Craven, banished
from Britain by her husband, traveled through Europe, Russia,
and Turkey in the 1780s, a period of significant but temporary
liberality. Her book, *Journey Through the Crimea to Constantinople*,
appeared in the form of missives to the Margrave of Anspach,
whom she addressed as "dear brother," but who was actually her
lover. In this book, she established herself as an outspoken critic of female dress and customs wherever
she went, never fearing to deprecate even the most
insignificant of faults.

*Lady Elizabeth Craven.*
George Romney, artist. Paston, *Little Memoirs*, 1901, facing p. 136.

While in Constantinople in 1786, Craven was a guest of the French ambassador, Comte de Choiseul-Gouffier, and, according to her own account, was much feted by the European community. Of her visit to the wife of the "Capitan Pacha," she came away with the impression that the women of that harem had worked hard to eradicate the gifts of beauty that nature had given them. The bathing and dressing up the Turkish women so loved were, she declared, "strange pastimes!"[42]

German novelist Countess Ida von Hahn-Hahn chronicled her visits to Egypt, Jerusalem, and Constantinople in several books, including *Orientalische Briefe, Letters from the Orient*, 1844. Although from an aristocratic family, she wrote novels, poems, and especially travel books to support herself, and her life, like Craven's, was imbued with the whiff of scandal. She was not only liberal in her politics, she was divorced and traveled with a lover, Baron von Bystram, with whom she had a son. And, like Craven, she voiced her opinions openly. As one reviewer wrote, "This lady commits the mistake of saying all she thinks."[43]

In 1850, following Bystram's death, Hahn-Hahn, a Protestant, converted to Catholicism, founded a convent, and renounced her earlier works.

FOLLOWING PAGES:
*"English in Cairo:*
*Visiting the Howling*
*Dervishes in the Mosque*
*of Mohammed Ali."* Drawing
by W. H. Overend, *Illustrated London*
*News*, 4 February 1893, 148–49.

*Is it the climate or the costume I wonder that makes the English maids ravish the Arab men so continually?*—Lucie Duff Gordon, 1865

# Western Women, Eastern Men
## FRIENDSHIP & LOVE

LUCIE DUFF GORDON was justifiably exasperated with amorous maids; her own, thirty-year-old Sally Naldrett, had just given birth to a baby fathered by Lucie's dragoman, Omar Abu Halawy. Sally's indiscretion created no small stir among Lucie's Egyptian friends, and stories of other flirts in service soon surfaced. One guide swore that he would never take on a party of lady travelers, as ladies inevitably had maids, and maids were guaranteed trouble, whether one succumbed to their advances or not. As Lucie observed, something in Egypt caused these maids to forget their places and misbehave.★

Englishwoman Jane Digby, who had her share of affairs while traveling through Europe and Syria in the 1840s and '50s, was peeved by her maid, Eugénie, who, it turned out, was flexing her own unaccustomed independence by sleeping with Jane's Macedonian lover, Xristodolous Hadji-Petros, and possibly with another lover, Syrian Sheikh al-Barak. Eugénie donned men's clothing, just as Jane did, and she, too, rode astride. She must have sensed that their mode of travel had elevated her status, certainly not to equal that of her mistress, but at least to a level of

*Ahmed Hassanein, Rosita Forbes's partner to Al-Kufrah, Libya, in 1921. Hassanein, The Last Oases, 1925, frontispiece.*

★Lucie Duff Gordon's letters home were published in *Letters from Egypt* and *Last Letters from Egypt*. Her references to Sally's pregnancy, however, remained unpublished until 1969.

greater importance than she had experienced in Europe, where other servants would continually reinforce her subordinate position.[1]

Aside from maids—and aside from Jane Digby, for that matter—most women travelers behaved impeccably, at least where their love lives were concerned, but it didn't mean they weren't attracted to the men they encountered.

Western women dealt directly and frequently with Eastern men, especially with innkeepers, caravan escorts, janissaries (Turkish soldiers), locally appointed consuls, and above all their dragomans, with whom they traveled for extended periods of time. The level of camaraderie that women were able to achieve with these men must have surprised both parties. In their accounts, women often described in detail the individual men they met, naming them and bringing to life their personalities and backgrounds, whereas their depictions of women tended to remain superficial.

In going to the East, women were freed of the social constraints they were accustomed to at home. In their daily transactions, they negotiated the rental of boats, the hiring of guides, and the transport of luggage. They tried out unaccustomed phrases in foreign languages and were praised for their efforts. And, as Princess Cristina di Belgiojoso discovered, men questioned them about world affairs and took their opinions seriously.

Women acted of their own accord; they made their own decisions about where they were going and how, and those decisions were not questioned just because a woman had made them. That they held their own purse strings was an important factor.

Western women were like nothing Eastern men had ever seen before. Although undeniably females in the physical sense, just by traveling they were judged to be outlandishly independent. By riding fearlessly, they were esteemed for their masculine accomplishments. And their clothing, a hodgepodge of feminine and masculine articles, tossed them into the category of some

*"Ascent of the Great Pyramid."* C. Rudolf Huber, artist. Ebers, *L'Égypte*, vol. 1, 1883, 149.

mystifying sex, neither man nor woman.

Emily Beaufort's experience in Palestine in 1859 illustrates the confusion some women could cause. A large crowd, attracted by her sketching, argued about whether she was "man or woman—'welled' or 'bint.'" She recounted that when she "stood up and they saw how small I was and my long riding-habit, besides the hat which they admired greatly, they seemed overcome with astonishment; but they agreed then that I must be a 'bint,' not a 'welled.'" Beaufort had con-

*Hester Stanhope in her full Turkish regalia.* Attributed to R. J. Hamerton. Meryon, *Memoirs of the Lady Hester Stanhope,* vol. 1, 1846, frontispiece.

founded them with both her activity and her appearance.[2]

Lady Hester Stanhope reveled in the impression that she made on Turkish dignitaries in Constantinople: "When did four Turks . . . visit and dine with a Christian woman? I wore my sword with such an air that it has made a conquest of them all, they begin to find their own women rather stupid, at least they say so, but men fib sadly." Stanhope's vanity, already astonishing, flourished. She wrote that "the Turks also estimate a person by their *riding* well or ill; and never having seen a woman ride out of a foot's pace, or ride the scampering horse of a great Pacha, they argue that I must be something very extraordinary indeed."[3]

For a woman all too used to deferring to men in most aspects of her life, this venture into the land of near sexlessness would have been exhilarating. Belgiojoso, a woman whose own independence had been bought with personal wealth, deemed it dangerous, especially for the young:

> I don't see how such travel, executed on camels in desert countries and among Arabs, could contribute to forming the heart and soul of these young women destined to live in another hemisphere, in the middle of a completely different society or civilization, nor help them to become obsequious girls, faithful wives or good mothers.[4]

Through travel, a woman might escape her society for perhaps a month, perhaps a year, but at some point she had to return home. Belgiojoso knew that readjustment to European life would be difficult, if not impossible, and that a young woman faced unhappiness at resuming her restricted life or would be compelled to defy her society and live as an outcast. Isabel Burton agreed, saying, "The Orient life unfit[ted] yourself for that of Europe."[5]

## SEX APPEAL

*The charm of the [Baghdad] bazars lies in the variety of race and costume and in the splendid* physique *of the greater number of the men. The European looks "nowhere."*—Isabella Bird, 1891[6]

There was also an unquestionable physical attraction. The clothing worn by men before European styles were adopted in the early twentieth century was considered dashing and wild. Turbans added height to already imposing figures; a multicolored sash, wrapped tightly around the middle, emphasized admirably proportioned physiques. The mustaches, black eyes, and rich skin tones of Syrian men compelled Gustave Flaubert to exclaim that if he were a woman, he would "go to Damascus for a pleasure trip!" Belgiojoso recognized the beauty but dismissed the intellect, declaring the men's faces to be empty of everything but "lively, powerful expressions of brutal passion."[7]

Alexine Tinne, in the Libyan desert in 1869, wrote that a troop of men dressed in robes and riding racing camels made a "blood-stirring scene, and if they came to Europe so in full glory I am sure the heart of many a young girl would beat for the handsome Tuareg, barbarians as they are, and many a youth would long to join them!" In southern Egypt, Lucie Duff Gordon shared sherbet with "handsome jet-black men, with features as beautiful as those of the young Bacchus." She added that they "described the distant lands in a way which would have charmed Herodotus."[8]

With their scanty clothing, Nubian sailors on the Nile drew further attention to the male body, especially when they stripped naked to dive from their boats. On this subject, Valérie de Gasparin wrote:

For myself, who has the happiness to be short sighted, I'm perhaps a bad judge of this business. However, I find that modesty suffers less to see a totally black Nubian in the water than to contemplate one hundred suggestive statues dazzling in their whiteness, lined up in the full sun along the galleries of Rome or of Naples. And yet, those women, who will swoon over a Nubian swimming, I've seen walking about with their eyes fully open in the middle of the Academies![9]

A Mme Fagnani, in Constantinople around 1875, was agog at the sultan's bodyguard

*"The Dragoman of Mr Moore, English Consul at Beyrout," 1841. Wilkie also sketched Mrs Moore (see page 71). Wilkie, Sir David Wilkie Sketches, 1843, pl. 14.*

dressed in the most gorgeous native costume that mind could invent, or money procure. Albanians who might have stood as models for Apollo, or Jupiter Olympus, adorned with snowy fustanelles [knee-length, pleated skirts], velvet jackets glittering with gold embroidery, pistols and sabers . . . moved amid the crowd as if they felt themselves to be of the god-like race of Hellas. Bedouins from the desert wrapped in the picturesque burnoose, Druses and Maronites, Smyrniotes and Armenians,

David Wilkie 1841

&c. Mr Moore English Consul at Beyrout

Greek and Turk, Mohammedan and Christian, came and went, all clothed in the most magnificent dresses that could be purchased.[10]

This awe easily survived closer inspection. The Burtons often socialized with the celebrated Algerian rebel leader Abd al-Qadir in Damascus in 1869. Isabel, a connoisseur of masculine good looks, judging from her single-minded pursuit of her dashing husband, Richard, was effusive in her praise of al-Qadir:

> A broad brow, with marked straight eyebrows, large dark-brown eyes, bright and piercing, but full of softness and intelligence; a complexion not a sickly olive, but a lively, warm brown, combine to make a handsome face. He has a Grecian nose, a delicately carved but firm mouth, a broad chin, and two rows of bright teeth; his hands and his whole personal appearance show blood, and his dignified bearing and cool self-possession are characteristics of his life . . . if you see him on horseback without knowing him to be Abd el Kadir, you would single him from a million, let the others be ever so brilliant . . . His mind is as beautiful as his face; he is every inch a Sultan.[11]

Isabel spent many peaceful evenings on Damascus rooftops, enraptured by the erudite conversations held between Abd al-Qadir, Richard, and Jane Digby, each switching between a multitude of languages with great facility.

Olympe Audouard was also impressed with Abd al-Qadir after traveling through a sandstorm with him in Egypt. She thought him to be "a superior man; he is very intelligent, with a just, lively and brilliant spirit; he has a very amiable character, something of dignity and of benevolence which charms. His bearing is noble and proud, and he is handsome still." To her, Abd al-Qadir embodied Eastern graciousness of manner and language.[12]

## Unaccustomed Respect

*I never knew what politeness was till I met with Turks.*—Lady Mary Elgin, 1799[13]

A good part of the attraction that Eastern men had for Western women was their courtesy. Even in everyday dealings, Eastern men showed an unparalleled deference that delighted and astonished, whereas a European stranger heaping similar praise upon a countrywoman would be suspected of ulterior motives.

*Abd al-Qadir.*

E. Ronjat, artist. Lortet, *Tour du monde* 44: 1882, 384.

Olympe Audouard lapped up all compliments, and her conviction that she warranted special treatment is evident throughout her book *Les Mystères de l'Égypte dévoilés*. Upon parting from a Bedouin sheikh, with whom she had dined, she was told that her visit was an honor and that, as the flower leaves a sweet and subtle perfume, she had left behind an equally sweet and lasting memory. "A Parisian couldn't find a more lovely thing to say," she declared.[14]

Lady Mary Wortley Montagu was also pleased with the attentions she received from her host, Achmet Bey, in Adrianople. "He has been educated in the most polite eastern learning ... You cannot imagine how much he is delighted with the liberty of conversing with me." Achmet Bey may indeed have been delighted with the conversation, but it was clearly Lady Mary who benefited from the liberty. She used the opportunity to discuss Eastern literature and customs, especially the confinement of women, which he assured her allowed them to confidently cheat on their husbands.[15]

Most women admired the manners displayed by Eastern men without interpreting their gestures and words to be more than courtesy demanded by the culture. Hester Stanhope praised the Bedouin for being even more polite than Turks. During her trip through southern Turkey in 1905, Gertrude Bell admitted to having "fallen a hopeless victim to the Turk; he is the most charming of mortals." Belgiojoso recognized that the politeness was offered because "a Muslim would never console himself for having forgotten the laws of hospitality." Louisa Jebb and her friend X were treated as "princesses whose hands and feet are kissed, whose word is law." These examples show that their activities brought them in regular contact with Eastern men.[16]

The sensitivity displayed by many Eastern men may have occasionally led women to lower their guard and accept more attention than they would normally tolerate. Pierre Loti, in Cairo in 1908, watched a group of some twenty tourists riding on mules, each with an attendant. Trailing at the rear was

> [a mature woman] so far as can be judged in the moonlight, but nevertheless still sympathetic to her driver, who, with both hands, supports her from behind on her saddle, with a touching solicitude that is peculiar to the country . . . This good lady evidently belongs to that extensive category of hardy explorers who, despite their high respectability at home, do not hesitate, once they are landed on the banks of the Nile, to supplement their treatment by the sun and the dry winds with a little of the "Bedouin cure."[17]

## DRAGOMANS

*I hope if I die away from you all,*
*you will do something for Omar*
*for my sake, I cannot con-*
*ceive what I should do*
*without his faithful and*
*loving care.*—Lucie
Duff Gordon, 1865[18]

*A resident of Alexandria*
*with her attendant.* Leopold
Carl Müller, artist. Ebers, *L'Égypte,*
vol. 1, 1883, 49.

Western women often
befriended their escorts,
whether dragomans, janis-
saries, or guides. They relied
on these men to take them
safely through countryside
that was, if not dangerous, at
least unfamiliar. In Europe, they
would have traveled in carriages, transported from
one post house to the next by a relay of anony-
mous drivers. Their fellow passengers would have
changed frequently, and there would have been
no time or opportunity to make friends. The
European *vetturino,* an escort hired for the duration of a trip,
would have been the closest equivalent to the dragoman, but
even he would not have taken care of all the little details that a
dragoman handled.

Marianne-Elisa de Lamartine, who left her husband idling in
Jaffa while she made a pilgrimage to Jerusalem, was touched by
the care her escort gave her. His admiration of her riding skills
went straight to her head. She wrote that "we have much to be
thankful for the extreme attention of [our] janissary and of his
exquisite politeness. Constantly occupied with the Arab mare
that I rode, he seemed frightened that I chanced jumping with
her and couldn't believe that I was able to maintain my balance
on the steep trails that we climbed." She added, "The respect of

*"Off for the Petrified Forest." Grace Thompson Seton on Adelia (center), "the Poet" on George Washington (right), and their dragoman, Shehata, on Abe Lincoln (left).*

Seton, A Woman Tenderfoot in Egypt, 1923, facing p. 162.

the Muslims for European women contrasts singularly with the subordination in which they hold their own."[19]

Lucie Duff Gordon overheard her dragoman, Omar, praising her and her daughter Janet Ross—then the London *Times* correspondent in Alexandria —to another Egyptian, Seleem Effendi:

By my soul, [Janet] rides like a Bedawee (Beduin), she shoots with the gun and pistol, and rows the boat; she speaks many languages, works with the needle like an Efreet, and to see her hands run over the teeth of the music-box (keys of piano) amazes the mind, while her singing gladdens the soul . . . And as to my lady, there is nothing that she does not know. When I feel my stomach tightened, I go to the divan and say to her, "Do you want anything, a pipe, or sherbet, or so and so?" and I talk till she lays down her book and talks to me, and I question her and amuse my mind, and, by God! if I were a rich man and could marry one English hareem like that I would stand before her and serve her like her mameluke.[20]

Omar surprised Duff Gordon by frankly describing how he missed his wife. She told him that the English would be shocked by his language. (Of course, she was too circumspect to repeat his exact words.) He replied that he would never speak in such a way to an Englishman, but to a woman such intimate talk was fine.[21]

Isabel Burton praised the bravery and attentiveness of her dragoman, Mulhem Wardi. Believing that she had a special relationship with all the dragomans of her acquaintance, she was stung to the quick when Hannah Misk, dragoman for the British consulate in Damascus, pointedly ignored her after Richard had been ignominiously dismissed as consul.[22]

*Lady travelers with their dragoman at the Pyramids in Egypt, c. 1910.*

Amelia Edwards's constant companion on her sketching excursions was Salame, a member of her *dhahabiya* crew. She depended on him to shade her with an umbrella, to fill her water bottle, and to hold her paint box. But he was more than just an escort or a servant; she described him as "young, active, intelligent, full of fun, hot-tempered withal, and as thorough a gentleman as I have ever had the pleasure of knowing." Salame's steady presence gave Edwards the confidence to go about otherwise unaccompanied.[23]

Louisa Jebb had a soft spot for the men who escorted her and her friend X through Turkey and Iraq. As their dragoman, Hassan, was with them for nearly seven months, the two

women certainly had time to get to know him. Jebb declared that his title of "dragoman" was a misnomer, as he spoke only Turkish. She called him their splendid "figure-head . . . as straight as a die and as supple as a willow, with a handsome head set well back on strong shoulders." Hassan confessed that he thought of Jebb as a child, and, because they had about fifty words in common, Jebb called their friendship a "silent" one. She greatly appreciated his absolute disdain for the trappings of civilization. When they parted at journey's end, Jebb admitted she had a lump in her throat.[24]

In our democratic age, we might be inclined to think of a woman and her dragoman as employer and employee and not question the camaraderie. But at that time, whether the woman was from the aristocracy or the middle class, she would have treated her employees as servants, and European servants who became friends with their mistresses were rare. A governess or nanny had a chance of lifelong intimacy with her charges, but other help was kept at arm's length. That dragomans were spoken of with warmth and respect meant that somehow barriers had been demolished and that women could be friends with them without restriction. Both parties knew that the relationship was temporary and without obligations, but all the same, numerous women made a point of recommending their dragomans to fellow travelers.

## THE EASTERN VIEW

*I have devoted much time and many journeys to working for the Arabs. Therefore, a number of their wise men have received me, pitying my sex, but willing, temporarily, to ignore it.*—Rosita Forbes, 1928[25]

Of the women surveyed here, Rosita Forbes comes across as one of the more levelheaded in her relationships with Eastern men. But if others are to be believed, Eastern men either fell all over

*Hassan, dragoman to Louisa Jebb and X. Jebb, By Desert Ways to Baghdad, 1908, facing p. 288.*

themselves to be near Western women or cursed them as unwelcome infidels.

Most responses from the men themselves have been related by Western writers. Charles Meryon, Hester Stanhope's physician, was told that Turks disliked the ruddy color of Englishwomen. Apparently, a certain number, left behind in Egypt after England's defeat of Napoleon, had been taken captive. "Their new masters washed them and washed them, hoping to get the brick-dust out of their cheeks; and, when they found it impossible they sent them about their business. Black women, the Turks said, they knew and liked, and white ones; but red women they never heard of till then." One can only presume that the poor things were badly sunburned.*[26]

In Egypt with the French military, Regula Engel, the wife of one of Napoleon's officers, wrote about the other women who had accompanied their husbands. Half of the wives, she claimed, made their graves in Egypt. One in particular had died by a swift stroke of her jealous husband's saber, because Egyptians, apparently, had welcomed her advances. "A Parisienne," observed Engel, "she had lived for nothing but men, scornful not of Copts, Turks, or even Mamelukes."[27]

If French poet Gerard de Nerval is to be believed, Egyptian men in the 1840s were repulsed by the exposed face, "completely naked, not only to those who want to see it, but to those who don't." Nerval's informant, Soliman-Aga, was appalled that the women he saw "in the streets, look at me with passionate eyes, and some even go so far as to want to kiss me." He went on to say that "[European women] are winter plants, without colour and without taste, with unhealthy faces tortured by hunger, because they barely eat . . . And as for marrying them,

---

* The presence of Englishwomen at Rosetta, in Egypt, in the early 1800s was confirmed by an eyewitness, guidebook writer Edward Clarke. He wrote that they "offered a singular contrast to the appearance exhibited by the *Arab* females." Women from India had also accompanied the Indian Army. Clarke suspected that the three groups—Egyptian, English, and Indian—"regarded the other two as so many savages; and who shall say which was the most refined."[28]

*Louisa Jebb, "Entertaining the Mudie at Nicaea."*

Jebb, By Desert Ways to Baghdad, 1908, facing p. 42.

that's something else; they are so badly brought up that it would be war and calamity in the house."[29]

Gustave Flaubert, however, in Egypt in 1849 and 1850, noted a measure of veneration towards European women: "Our guide took us by the hand and led us with great mystery to show us the imprint on the sand of the boot of a woman. It was an Englishwoman's, who had been there a couple of days previous. Poor fellow!"[30]

Flaubert himself did not think much of the Englishwomen he had seen in Egypt, especially those he had shared a boat with from Alexandria to Cairo. As historian Anthony Sattin discovered, there is a good chance these women were Florence Nightingale and her older companion, Mrs Selina Bracebridge. Flaubert thought them horrible and mocked the elder woman for sporting an unflattering green eyeshade.[31]

If Nightingale had noticed any disagreeable Frenchmen, she didn't mention them in her diary, but she did comment on Arab hostility. She chose an especially controversial place to test her presence: the El Azhar mosque in Cairo, where she and Mrs Bracebridge were treated like "Christian female dogs":

As to the Mahometan horror of us, I never could feel anything but the deepest sympathy for it, the deepest humiliation at exciting it. When you think that a woman who goes with her face uncovered is, with them, more indecent than a woman who should go without clothes among us—that it is here the stamp of a disgraced character—it is exactly as if a dancer were to come, in her disgraceful dress, into Salisbury Cathedral . . . I only wonder at the tolerance with which we are treated here, not at the contrary—but it makes an European woman's life in the East a misery.[32]

As we have seen, Lucie Duff Gordon wrote of the mutual admiration between her and the Egyptian men she encountered. She received some insight into their thinking when she asked about a young Egyptian woman who had passed through Luxor. El Hággeh, "the Pilgrimess," was eighteen years old, and, though clearly female, she wore men's clothes and wandered alone freely. When Duff Gordon asked why no one took exception to El Hággeh's liberty, her captain replied, " 'Why

not? if she does not wish to marry, she can go alone; if she does, she can marry—what harm? She is a virgin and free.'" In other words, being unattached meant—in the minds of the citizens of Luxor, at any rate—that she had no need to curtail her behavior to protect her husband's reputation. The unaccompanied European woman may have generated a similar response from some men.[33]

Lacking firsthand statements from Eastern men, one can only take these disparate observations at face value and conclude that some women adapted well and others did not, just as some Eastern men were tolerant and others less so. Few women, however, reported disagreeable one-on-one encounters with Eastern men.

*"The Sheikh" (left) and "The Sheikh's Donkey" (right). Miss Gushington, robbed of her dress, frightens a venerable sheikh into thinking she's an ifrit, evil spirit, by displaying her crinoline. This delightful story by Lord Dufferin lampooned lady travelers to the East.* Dufferin, editor, Lispings from Lower Latitudes, 1863, pl. XV and XVI.

## Living Together

*Was he not my husband in all but name?*—Margaret Fountaine, 1903[34]

Proposals of marriage from Eastern men were not unheard of. Before her ignominious pregnancy, Sally, Lucie Duff Gordon's maid, was sought as a bride for the son of the wealthy Mustapha Aga. "He said of course she would keep her own religion and her own customs . . . I said she was too old, but they think that no objection at all . . . Fancy Sally as Hareem of the Sheykh-el-Beled of Luxor!" Lucie concluded that such an offer showed "that the Arabs draw no unfavorable conclusions as to our morals from the freedom of our manners." In other words, the European woman was not seen to exploit her liberty by indulging in vice.[35]

Lucie was also the recipient of a proposal from a "very handsome" sheikh. Omar, her go-between, told the sheikh she was married and besides, her hair had gone gray. No matter, her suitor replied, she could get divorced and dye her hair. His admiration for her old-fashioned qualities and learning—so unlike modern Egyptian women, he claimed—drove him to declare that for her an honorable man would gladly kill or be killed.[36]

Just how much serious courtship was there between Western women and Eastern men? The difficulty in tracking down examples is, in part, the result of the travelers' reticence, so unlike today's writers of tell-all memoirs. What we know comes from third-party accounts and from private diaries, never intended for others' eyes.

Jane Digby, a keeper of such diaries—the more revealing sections of which were written in code—had several Bedouin lovers during her first year in Syria in 1853–54. Margaret Fountaine, who lived with her Syrian dragoman, prohibited the opening of her journals until long after her death. Isabelle Eberhardt's

*Medjuel al-Mezrab.*
Carl Haag, artist. *Illustrated London News,*
16 July 1870, p. 57.

frank confessions of her promiscuity and her affair with and
subsequent marriage to Algerian Slimène Ehnni were relegated
to her diaries and to short stories published posthumously.[37]

Jane, whose romantic life has been ably chronicled in Mary
S. Lovell's biography *Rebel Heart,* was originally married to
Lord Ellenborough. She spurned the security of this union by
following her first—or perhaps second—lover, a German
diplomat, to the Continent. The succession of lovers that followed included a German count, whom she married, King
Ludwig I of Bavaria, and Macedonian rebel leader Xristodolous
Hadji-Petros. She bore six children, possibly one of which was
her first husband's.

After living off and on in Greece for over a decade, Digby
ended up in Damascus in 1853, at the age of forty-six. While
there, she made plans to go to Palmyra, a very difficult journey
at that time, especially for a woman. Her escort was Medjuel
al-Mezrab, of the Anazeh tribe. During that year, she had affairs
with Saleh, a Bedouin who conducted her through Palestine,
and Sheikh al-Barak, with whom she went to Baghdad, but, in
the interval, Medjuel asked her to marry him.

Medjuel's main drawback as a potential husband was his
wife, Maascha. By March 1855, Medjuel had divorced Maascha,
and he and Jane were married. Jane threw herself into Bedouin
life. She traveled frequently between Damascus and Palmyra,
learned how to survive in the desert, and impressed skeptical
members of Medjuel's tribe with her horsemanship and wis-
dom. She also maintained a beautiful home in Damascus. Her
circle of European friends included the Burtons, the Blunts, and
sisters Emily and R.E.* Beaufort.

Isabel Burton was repulsed by Medjuel's dark skin but admitted that "he was a very intelligent and charming man," if you
didn't think of him as a potential husband.[38] Emily Beaufort was
more impressed, praising his dress, chivalrous manners, and above

---

*Emily Beaufort did not name her sister and traveling companion in her book
*Egyptian Sepulchres and Syrian Shrines.*

all his care of her and her sister while they were out in the desert. All in all, she portrayed a man well worth marrying:

> He is—like *all true* Bedouins—a small man, about five feet three inches in height, slightly made, but erect, very graceful in all his motions, and with a light, easy step; his face is really beautiful—of a perfect oval—a long aquiline nose, delicately formed mouth, small regular teeth of dazzling whiteness, and large black eyes that could be soft and sweet as any woman's, or flash with a fierce, wild, eagle glance that really made one start.[39]

Margaret Fountaine's Eastern romance began in 1901, when she was thirty-one. She had been traveling on her own for a decade, following a disastrous, one-sided infatuation with an Irish chorister. The end of this unfortunate obsession launched her on a new life, one that would hone her skills as a passionate collector of butterflies and eventually take her around the world.

*Beirut, c. 1900. Margaret Fountaine hinted in her diary that something had happened during her stay here in 1901 that had made her realize she could never be "the wife of a good man."* [40]

Beirut. Port.
Beyrouth. Le port.

After roaming Europe in entomological pursuits, catching gentlemen's glances and furtive kisses as well, she went to Syria. There she met Khalil Neimy, a Syrian dragoman seven years her junior. The romance started out badly. She was unsettled by his advances; then, after nearly succumbing, she fled back to England. Following a two-year interlude of confusion about whether or not he was married (he was) and several anxious trips between England and Syria, she went to Constantinople, resolving to do no more than to hire him again as her dragoman. Once they became lovers, their travels together began, ending only with Neimy's death in 1929.[41]

Fountaine's massive butterfly collection was bequeathed to the Castle Museum in Norwich, along with her meticulously illustrated journals, which had been sealed with instructions that they were to remain so until 1978. When they were finally opened, her exuberant and restless life was revealed; two volumes have been published from them: *Love Among the Butterflies* and *Butterflies and Late Loves,* 1986.

Isabelle Eberhardt's experiences in Algeria, though just outside the geographical area covered here, illustrate the deep passion that European women could feel for the East. Love of the vast and empty expanses of the desert may have influenced her as much as the opportunities for sexual freedom. Eberhardt, a writer of Russian origins who was raised in Switzerland, spent a good part of the years between 1897 and her death in 1904 in Algeria. She converted to Islam, called herself "Si Mahmoud," and wore men's clothing, both European and Algerian, as it suited her. In spite of her ambiguous sexual identity, she took Algerian lovers, and one, Slimène Ehnni, an officer in the Algerian French Army, became her enduring companion, and then, after many obstacles were cleared, her husband. Their affair, which began in the desert town of El Oued, had the air of Saharan romances later depicted in novels.[42]

Ehnni left the army and they married. Their passion, so strongly dependent on the desert and freedom, was sapped by mundane town life. They spent increasing periods of time apart, as Isabelle continued to submit to her wanderlust. When she died in a flash flood in the Algerian town of Aïn Sefra in 1904, they had been briefly reunited after a separation of eight months.

So many women became entangled in cross-cultural romantic complications that in 1899, Reverend Charles Butcher of Cairo sent a letter to the *Times* in London, warning Englishwomen who responded to advertisements for governesses placed by Egyptians to confirm the validity of the ad first, either with him or with one of his fellow ministers. Although he believed most advertisers to be legitimate, others threatened ruin:

*Isabelle Eberhardt dressed as a sailor in 1895.*
Louis David, photographer. Stéphan, *Isabelle Eberhardt ou la révélation du Sahara*, 1930, frontispiece.

Total ignorance of the country, its people, language, and customs, the isolation more or less necessitated by the system of harem life . . . combined with the new and strange moral atmosphere in which the newcomer suddenly finds herself—all these causes too often contribute to bring about, almost unconsciously, the final result, a woman's life disastrously wrecked. Even if, as is sometimes the case, promises of marriage are freely made, it should be borne in mind that, should the promise be fulfilled—a somewhat improbable contingency in most instances—the husband can at any moment free himself, by the facile system of Moslem divorce, from the bond into which he has entered, leaving the woman practically unprovided for, but still, in the eyes of the law of her own country, a wedded wife.[43]

Butcher's wife, Edith, the former Miss Floyer, first went to
Egypt in 1878 with her brother. In *Egypt as We Knew It,* she
described the many pitfalls of cross-cultural marriage, to her the
most important of which was uncertain legal status. A woman
of her acquaintance who had married a Muslim was refused a
divorce under English law because the courts did not recognize
her marriage to a member of a polygamous community.[44]

Whereas a man could marry outside his country without
change in status, a woman faced loss of citizenship. Twelve years
after her marriage, Jane Digby discovered that she had lost hers.
Margaret Fountaine, who considered marrying Neimy, was told
of another Englishwoman who had married a Syrian only to be
informed that in doing so she had relinquished her citizenship.
"Merely another instance of the injustice of the laws concern-
ing women in this world," Fountaine observed.[45]

Public opinion about women who married Eastern men
was divided. Some regarded Jane Digby's life as the height of
romance. Emily Beaufort, befriending her in 1859, treated her
situation as one needing the utmost discretion; Jane's name
never appears in Beaufort's book. Most, however, were appalled
and avoided Jane, or engaged in vicious gossip. J. L. Porter, the
author of *Murray's Hand-Book to Syria and Palestine,* admonished
writers who "garnished" their travel books with Jane's "sad and
singular history . . . One would have supposed that men of education might have found enough of objects among the classic
ruins of Greece, and the sacred sites of Syria, wherewith to
amuse and instruct their readers, without raking up the wrongs
and the misfortunes of an unhappy Englishwoman."[46]

Having heard much about Jane, French traveler Raphaël
Bernoville had high expectations when he met her in 1865, but
he wound up feeling sorry for her. He had been maliciously
informed that it was only her great wealth that kept Medjuel
from discarding her. "What was most incomprehensible," he
wrote, "was the obstinacy with which she strove to prove to us
that she had found happiness, vaunting the charms of the desert
and of the Oriental nights." Nonetheless, he admired "the

energy with which this singular woman should be blessed with to resist the infinite number of fatigues and almost incredible dangers that she risked."[47]

Isabel Burton cautioned young Englishwomen to beware of faux Syrian princes. Too many were falling under the spell of these pretenders and were deluded enough to consider marrying them. "Amir Mulhim Rustam is the only real 'Prince of the Lebanon' left," declared Isabel. "So remember his name; for unless he goes over to England to look for a wife you will not be Princesses of the Lebanon." She continued:

> At any rate, insist upon going to Syria before the fatal knot is tied, and see your future home and family. Then, if it is a real affection, carry out your romantic project, and be prepared to suffer for it. If you see a Syrian with a handsome face pervading society in a green and gold jacket, and wearing a fez, admire the costume, and be hospitable and kind to the wearer, but do not fall in love and marry . . . The life is so different; you must lose your English independence, and sink to the level of the Eastern rule for women.[48]

Ella Sykes, in Persia in 1895, received a visit from some Kerman women, who warned her "earnestly not to enter into the state of wedlock with a Persian, as their marriage customs were *khaili kharah* (very bad)." Sykes assured them she had no plans to tie the knot, but they could not understand that a woman might be content to remain unmarried.[49]

Gertrude Bell, visiting Aleppo in 1905, was surprised to learn that the wife of Aleppan Muhammad Ali Pasha was a "pleasant little lady from Brixton." Bell believed the couple were happy, but she could not "as a general rule recommend Turkish pashas as husbands to the maidens of Brixton." Bell went on to observe that though the lady was able to participate in European activities, she still had to conform to Eastern standards in order not to belittle her husband's status. She may have been exercising her freedom in choosing to live in the East and in her choice of husband, but she renounced it once she married.[50]

## A Home for Harlots?

*The Europeans nearly all arrive by the same route, viz., Odessa, Constantinople, Cairo and Port Said. After a few years in Bombay or Calcutta . . . they flit to Colombo and the Far East, where the sorry pilgrimage eventually closes.*—S. M. Edwardes, commissioner of police, Bombay, 1913[51]

Prostitutes form a somewhat neglected group of women travelers. Those working in the East came from many countries, including Britain, France, Italy, Malta, Cyprus, Poland, and Russia. Unfortunately, trying to obtain information about these women and their reasons for ending up where and as they did is virtually impossible. They were certainly attracted by the idea of steady work. With an abundance of French and British troops in Alexandria, for example, it is not surprising that, in 1923, of the city's 1,356 known prostitutes, a third were French.[52]

Even less is known about women who did not overtly work for money but who willingly slept with men in return for other favors. In the 1850s, Samuel Shepheard, the owner of Shepheard's Hotel in Cairo, discovered that his new housekeeper, Miss Carnes, formerly of Missirie's in Constantinople, expected to be his mistress as well. She was disabused of this notion—Sam was happily married—and was eventually fired because of an uncontrollable drinking habit.[53]

Then there were those who were simply rumored to be loose. Mme Rousillon, possibly the housekeeper at Cairo's French Hotel in the 1850s, was apparently found in the arms of a traveler, in his room with the door unbolted, wearing neither "sheet nor shirt." She was not dismissed.[54]

Lady Mary Elgin's letters to her mother were filled with gossip about loose ladies. In one report, she described Constantinople residents Mme Pisani and Baroness Hübsch as "*infamous, infamous.*" Elgin asked, "Are you not surprised at Mme Pisani? . . . She has had three or four intrigues, but who do you think was the last? You can never guess —— old —— ! There is hardly a woman here, there is not a history about." Disreputable Mme Pisani was the wife of Venetian Antonaki Pisani, chief dragoman to the English embassy.[55]

Several Saint-Simoniennes in Egypt in 1834–35, including Clorinde Rogé, Suzanne Voilquin, and Agarithe Caussidère, had affairs, though from all accounts only with Europeans. Caussidère, singled out as a prostitute who "went from tent to tent with excessive ease," was reproached for her lengthy visits with Soliman Pasha.[56]

Western literature has long connected the East with sexuality, and male travelers certainly tested this association for themselves. It is safe to conclude, however, that nineteenth-century women did not visit the East with the intention of exploring sexual opportunities, although a few admitted to having such encounters. Too many reasons, some obvious, others less so, prevented them from doing so. For a start, lofty Christian morals fortified most of them with a strong repugnance for adultery, promiscuity, and even such liberal social intercourse as dancing too often or talking too long with an unrelated man. As well, occasions to take advantage of opportunities were rare, privacy being a dear commodity for most travelers.

Another factor was the fear of pregnancy. Aristocratic women had ways and means of dealing with unwanted children, and poor women could keep them without loss of social status, but working- and middle-class women were destroyed by having an illegitimate baby.

No one was safe from venereal disease. Eberhardt was rumored to have passed on an "intimate infection" to an Algerian. But it was not until well into the twentieth century that any woman traveler admitted to safeguarding herself against VD. When Ella Maillart, Swiss author of *Turkestan Solo,* in central Asia in 1932, was warned against wandering off alone, she confessed to having packed some neosalvarsan, a medicine used for syphilis.[57]

Others, who may have been tempted by an affair in their native land, were prejudiced against anyone from outside their own social and ethnic milieu or were sensitive to others' prejudices. One did not have to travel far to find examples of such bias; even marrying someone from elsewhere in Europe could be frowned upon. For example, Englishwoman Hester Thrale, who respectably married an Italian in 1784, soon found herself ostracized from her own circle.

The East must have been an attractive place for those thinking of indulging in censurable behavior. The men were handsome, it was easy to develop friendships with them, and there were ostensibly fewer societal restrictions than at home. Western women, except for those who remained within the confines of European communities in cities such as Cairo or Constantinople, could easily evade their own society's critical gaze, especially if they were discreet. Isabel Burton noted, for example, that between nineteen and thirty Europeans lived in Damascus in 1869–70, three of whom were English. When Jane Digby arrived in 1853, that number would have been considerably less. Her marriage to Medjuel al-Mezrab was too audacious to be ignored, however, and drew much attention, even in faraway England. Both Digby and Isabelle Eberhardt might be admired today for their open defiance of their society's mores, but while they lived, they were subjected to suspicion and scorn.[58]

That Western women were able to make genuine, if short-lived, friendships with Eastern men was remarkable enough. These new comrades treated them with an equality that they had rarely experienced among their own menfolk. The addition of a good measure of Eastern respect and flattery gave them a sense that they had become honorary men, capable of achieving whatever they set out to do.

Engraved by C.H.Jeens.

## A SYMPATHETIC TRAVELER
Lucie Duff Gordon (1821–69)

In late 1862, Lucie Duff Gordon, a habituée of the smart, literary scene in London, left her beloved home and made her way to Alexandria, accompanied only by her maid, Sally Naldrett. Lucie was suffering from tuberculosis, or consumption, as it was then called, and escape from England's damp, cold climate was imperative if she were to live. She spent winters in Luxor, returning to Cairo in the hot months of summer. She became absorbed in daily life, took up Arabic lessons, distributed medication and advice, received both Egyptian and European visitors, and fought her ever-present illness.

Lucie was a keen observer of Egyptian customs and relished describing, in letters home, the high esteem in which Egyptian men held Englishwomen.

*Lucie Duff Gordon.* Duff Gordon, *Last Letters from Egypt*, 1875, frontispiece.

Egyptians, apparently, were appalled by the way Englishmen treated their wives, especially their lack of kindness to them and their manner of talking about them out loud. "An Arab," declared Lucie, "thinks himself a happy man if he can marry an English girl."[59]

She quickly shed what few European prejudices she may have had, along with the other trappings of her former life. In 1864, she wrote to her husband, Alexander, "It is now two months since I have worn stockings, and I think you would wonder at the fellaha who 'owns you', so deep a brown are my face, hands and feet." From this time until her death shortly

★ The *Maison de France* was built by British consul Henry Salt, then lived in by the Belzonis around 1817. It was taken over by the French, lent to a variety of travelers (including Flaubert and Maxime Du Camp), then rented to Duff Gordon. It was torn down sometime after 1880.

after her forty-ninth birthday, she lived in what was known as the *Maison de France,* the French House, a rambling edifice built into the Temple of Luxor.[60]

Amelia Edwards, when touring Luxor in 1874, nearly five years after Lucie's death, made a point of seeing the French House, recording her impressions in the manner of a pilgrim making a visit to a shrine. She noted the few bits of simple furniture and commented that "all was very bare and comfortless ...We were shocked at the dreariness of the place—till we went to the window. That window, which commanded the Nile and the western plain of Thebes, furnished the room and made its poverty splendid."[61]

Egypt's heat may not have saved Lucie Duff Gordon, but, judging from the humor and vigor that infuse her letters, it did relieve her dreadful symptoms. Her love for her Egyptian friends may have been even more effective, as they gave her life special meaning.

*Last night we were dirty, isolated, and free, to-night we are clean, sociable, and trammelled.*—Louisa Jebb, 1908

# The Journey's End

LOUISA JEBB checked into her fancy Damascus hotel, had a bath, and changed into clean clothes. After a half year spent traveling through remote stretches of Turkey and Mesopotamia, she felt woefully out of place. Proudly clutching her stained, torn, and much-mended coat, she knew, however, that she would always have her memories: a wild raft trip down the Tigris, a near robbery, a no-holds-barred savage dance in an Iraqi village, and the first magical glimpse of Palmyra's ruins after a long and arduous journey.

Jebb was about to resume her "trammelled" life, but she realized that she would never be the same. She wrote, "The essential facts of [desert countries] sink into you imperceptibly, until at the end they are so woven into the fibres of your nature that, even when removed from their influence, you will never quite lose them."[1]

In my introduction, I asked how, in going to the East, nineteenth- and early-twentieth-century women were able to find liberty. We have seen, from the examples of Louisa Jebb and others, that a woman who wished to do so could dress in non-restricting attire, readily associate with those of differing social strata, become friends with men,

*Louisa Jebb at a site with Hittite inscriptions. Hassan, her dragoman, stands next to her, on the right.* Jebb, By Desert Ways to Baghdad, 1908, facing p. 80.

and pursue her own interests, all activities that provoked criticism at home. As well, the challenges of moving about, of finding accommodation and food, and of adapting to a new culture and language helped sharpen her skills, thereby bolstering self-reliance and confidence.

The distance from one's own culture, both in miles traveled and in state of mind, contributed powerfully to this sense of freedom. In the absence of criticism from either sex, the traveler experienced the benefits and drawbacks of following her own road. And whatever the outcome, she became, as Isabel Burton wrote, "unfit" for her old life. Change was inevitable. If she were an Amelia Edwards or a Gertrude Bell, she tackled a new career; if a Lady Mary Wortley Montagu, she followed through on her avowal to live a free life; if a Hester Stanhope, Jane Digby, or Lucie Duff Gordon, she never went home. If she were any of a hundred others, she wrote up her experiences and planned even more ambitious trips.

Women could find freedom in some form in almost any region of the world, from the North American West to the Himalayas. The open road, the absence of expectations, a simple existence, and escape from society's constraints were not exclusive to the East. But not only was the East close geographically to Europe, it offered something more. Long associated with a compelling exoticism, this area was also characterized by liberating clothing, simple and genuine hospitality, and the apparent absence of the evils of progress.

The East was also distinguished by the seclusion in which the women lived, and visits to harems were a catalyst for Western women. Travelers from the eighteenth and early nineteenth century saw in the lives of their Eastern counterparts a freedom that they immediately envied and wished to emulate. Those who followed, especially after the 1830s, believed they themselves were much freer and, in comparing their lives, the importance of their own liberty—no matter how limited—became clearer.

Writing about travel transformed private thoughts into articulate observations. Whether an ordinary diary, circulated to friends and family, or a published book to be read by a wide audience, accounts by women travelers became increasingly popular. From 1839 until 1920, well over two hundred books by women about their Eastern travels appeared. Nearly all of them contain descriptions of harems, references to dragomans, explanations of the logistics of travel, and commentary on liberty. As the nineteenth century progressed, women pushed their travel writing into the realms of the humanities, social sciences, and exploration.

Periodicals regularly reviewed these books. The *Illustrated London News* declared Ida Pfeiffer, for example, to be "one of the most remarkable women of this or any other time. The record of her adventurous career reads like a story in the Arabian Nights." *Blackwood's* in 1896, critiquing Pfeiffer, Isabella Bird, and Alexine Tinne, to name those of interest here, remarked, "In such an age as this we need wonder at nothing that women will dare."[2]

These women challenged restrictions imposed on their liberty by traveling outside their societies. They experienced what it was like to be foreigners in distant lands, limited only by those constraints they put on themselves. In pushing these limits, they made their world—and ours—a vastly richer place.

# NOTES

INTRODUCTION: pages 1–5
Epigraph: Burton 1893, 483.
1  Burton 1879 [1875], 1.
2  Ibid., 2.
3  Hanson, 142–43.

SETTING THE STAGE: pages 7–31
Epigraph: Bell 1907, 1.
1  Searight, 124, 150; Waller, 804.
2  Sykes, 43.
3  Hahn-Hahn, *Orientalische Briefe,* quoted in Haja and Wimmer, 8.
4  Montagu, vol. 2, 51.
5  Pardoe, vol. 1, 3.
6  Duff Gordon 1983 [1902], 34.
7  Edwards, 3; Sykes, 3.
8  Burton 1893, 534n; 1879 [1875], 4.
9  Burton and Wilkins, 393.
10 Duff Gordon 1983 [1902], 29.
11 Pardoe, vol. 1, 3.
12 Edwards, 201.
13 Sykes, 3.
14 Forbes 1928, 16.
15 Asher, 248; Izzard, 125–26.
16 Forbin quoted in Manley, 189.
17 Poole quoted in *Blackwood's,* March 1845, 291.
18 "Women," 675; "Divorce," 264; Arnaud-Duc, 108, 109.
19 Brassey 1889, 288; Bell 1927, 258; Bell to Hugh Bell; Bell to Frank Balfour.
20 Saint-Simonien creed quoted in Ivray, 9.
21 Ivray, 144.
22 Edidin, 109; Ivray, 169, 186; Allemagne 1930, 430.
23 Allemagne 1930, 421.
24 Belgiojoso 1855: 3, 81.
25 Ibid., 1, 467; Colet 1986 [1859], 65.

LITTLE THINGS FEEL THE COLD: pages 33–63
Epigraph: Jebb, 14.
1  Ibid., 11.
2  Ibid., 123.
3  Ibid., 282–83.
4  Ibid., 13–14.
5  Blunt 1881, vol. 1, 229.
6  Jebb, 292.
7  Forbes 1928, 265.
8  Nisbet, 186: Mary and her husband later divorced, and Mary's letters were published under her maiden name, Nisbet; Stanhope quoted in [Meryon], *Travels,* vol. 2, 38.

9  Craven, 281.
10 Dieulafoy 1883, 160.
11 Edwards, 11–12.
12 Moon, 176: Brenda Moon's research uncovered the names of Edwards's European traveling companions, a detail that Edwards herself did not elaborate on; Edwards, 40–41.
13 Forbes 1928, 2.
14 Bird, Isabella, vol. 1, 128.
15 Ibid., 52.
16 Bell 1927, 231.
17 Ibid., 202.
18 Porter, vol. 1, 26.
19 Martineau, 399.
20 Belgiojoso 1855: 4, 1218–19.
21 Jebb, 14.
22 Ibid., 15.
23 Pfeiffer 1852, 41; 1851, 329–30.
24 Joanne and Isambert, 351; Hornby, 34.
25 Bird, Michael, 41–42; Shepheard quoted in Bird, Michael, 133.
26 Jebb, 277.
27 Ibid., 137–38.
28 Egerton, app. D; Wilkinson, 3–5; Stoddart, 224.
29 Belgiojoso 1855: 3, 61.
30 Bird, Isabella, vol. 1, 226.
31 Pfeiffer 1852, 90.
32 Stark 1951, 128–29.
33 Bell 1927, 212.
34 Forbes 1928, 60.
35 Bird, Isabella, vol. 2, 64.
36 Martineau, 339.
37 Tinne quoted in Gladstone, 209.
38 Gladstone, 202, 206, 220–22.
39 Trollope 1981 [1860], 60.
40 Trollope 1981 [1865], 29–30, 35, 37.
41 Pfeiffer 1852, 76.
42 Ibid.
43 Ross, 55.
44 Pfeiffer 1852, 128.
45 Ibid., 132.
46 Ibid., 328.
47 Bird, Isabella, vol. 1, 45.
48 Ibid., vol. 2, 125.
49 Perrot, 463.
50 Forbes 1928, 1.
51 Forbes 1921, 76.
52 Forbes 1928, 273.
53 Stark 1951, 62.
54 Ibid., 84, 86.

55  Ibid., 86.
56  Ibid., 188.

DRESSING EN AMAZONE: pages 65–85
Epigraph: Burton 1879 [1875], 174.
1   Rodenbeck, 67.
2   Edwards, 50: Beaufort, vol. 1, 115.
3   Sykes, 18.
4   Montagu, vol. 1, 372–73; vol. 2, 60, 70.
5   Fay, 80.
6   Nisbet, 65.
7   Lamartine, vol. 2, 48, 59.
8   Ibid., vol. 1, 130.
9   Martineau, 27, 256.
10  Lovell, 159, 202; Burton and Wilkins, 395.
11  Burton 1879 [1875], 65, 108.
12  Ibid., 108–109.
13  Gordon and Cross, 226n; *Times,* 3 August 1889, 5.
14  [Meryon], *Travels,* vol. 1, 193.
15  Stanhope quoted in Cleveland, 131.
16  Stanhope quoted in Manley, 184.
17  [Meryon], *Travels,* vol. 1, 299.
18  Allemagne 1930, 430.
19  Eberhardt, 59.
20  [Meryon], *Travels,* vol. 1, 108.
21  Ivray, 174–75.
22  Beaufort, vol. 2, 6.
23  Burton 1879 [1875], 175.
24  Ibid., 174.
25  Ibid., 110.
26  Ibid., 169.
27  Blunt 1881, vol. 1, 22; Bell quoted in Burgoyne, vol. 1, 235.
28  Bird, Isabella, vol. 1, 17.
29  Ibid., 132.
30  Bell 1907, X.
31  Thesiger quoted in Asher, 150.
32  Quote in Cunnington, 227.
33  [Meryon], *Travels,* vol. 1, 95, 99–100, 157–58.
34  Stanhope quoted in Cleveland, 127.
35  [Meryon], *Travels,* vol. 2, 176.
36  Ibid., 217; Bruce, 186–87.
37  Thomson, 81.

MORE THAN OCCUPIED: pages 87–107
Epigraph: Dieulafoy 1883, 91.
1   Dieulafoy 1887, 2.
2   Sackville-West, 138.
3   Dieulafoy 1887, 392–93.
4   Quoted from Sackville-West, 142.
5   Edwards, 354.
6   Ibid., xv.
7   Ibid., 310.
8   O'Neill, 171.
9   Blunt 1986, 244.
10  Finch, 54.

11  Bell quoted in Burgoyne, vol. 1, 304.
12  Burgoyne, vol. 1, 17.
13  Bell 1927, 218; Bell's photographs, diaries, and letters, both published and unpublished, are now held in the Gertrude Bell Archives at the University of Newcastle, UK.
14  Bell quoted in Burgoyne, vol. 1, 298; Bell 1927, 341–52.
15  Bell 1927, 258; Winstone, 112, 205.
16  Thesiger reference from Izzard, 31; Winstone, 162; Stark 1951, 88.
17  Stark 1953, 134; Bell quoted in Burgoyne, vol. 2, 233, 357.
18  Sackville-West, 60.
19  Audouard, 338.
20  "Bellicose," quoted from Augri and Leospo, 43.
21  Carré, vol. 2, 262–63; Audouard, 428, 430–34.
22  Audouard, 19.
23  Flaubert quoted in Steegmuller, 220.
24  Carré, vol. 2, 310, 314; Colet 1879, 203.
25  Gray, 345–52; Carré, vol. 2, 313.
26  Burton 1879 [1875], 181.
27  Ibid.
28  Ibid., 181–82.
29  Burton 1893, 470–71.
30  Burton 1879 [1875], 383.
31  Engel, 56.

THE LIBERATING VEIL: pages 109–33
Epigraph: Craven, 305.
1   Yeazell, 150.
2   Ibid., 2.
3   Belgiojoso 1855: 1, 474.
4   Gasparin, 362.
5   Craven, 295–96.
6   Pardoe, vol. 4, 127.
7   Craven quoted in Paston, 153.
8   Martineau, 236, 235.
9   Ibid., 236.
10  Audouard, 227.
11  Duff Gordon 1983 [1902], 308.
12  Belgiojoso 1855: 2, 1036.
13  Ibid., 1034, 1047.
14  Edwards, 480; Lovell, 240; Digby quoted in Lovell, 308; Lovell, 309.
15  Hahn-Hahn quoted in *Times,* 17 September 1845, 8; Audouard, 425; Martineau, 442.
16  Stanhope quoted in Cleveland, 133.
17  Martineau, 235.
18  Craven, 296.
19  Montagu, vol. 1, 374–75, 355–56.
20  Craven, 296.
21  Hahn-Hahn quoted in *Times,* 17 September 1845, 8.

22 Hornby, 57.
23 Ibid., 59.
24 Montagu, vol. 1, 357; Nisbet, 131.
25 Beaufort, vol. 2, 393.
26 Brassey 1880, pt. 1, 79.
27 Ibid.
28 Beaufort, vol. 2, 401.
29 Brassey 1880, pt. 2, 350.
30 Belzoni, 146, 151: Sarah Belzoni's account, titled *A Short Account of the Women of Egypt, Nubia, and Syria,* has sometimes been mistakenly referred to as *A Trivial Account* . . .
31 Gasparin, 88–89, 90.
32 Burton 1879 [1875], 108–109.
33 Brassey, quoted in Micklewright, 20.
34 Cleveland, 208; Asmar quoted in Cleveland, 215.
35 Gasparin, 329, 336, 346.
36 Dieulafoy 1883, 110.
37 The wife of a "high official" quoted in Dodd, 467–68.
38 Seton, 32.
39 Bell quoted in Burgoyne, vol. 2, 220–21.
40 Forbes 1928, 180, 182.
41 Montagu, vol. 2, 70.
42 Craven, 296.
43 [Eastlake], 131.

WESTERN WOMEN, EASTERN MEN: pages 137–69
Epigraph: Duff Gordon 1969 [1865], 187.
1 Lovell, 147, 179–80.
2 Beaufort, vol. 2, 20.
3 Stanhope quoted in Cleveland, 102, 146.
4 Belgiojoso 1858, 316–17.
5 Burton 1879 [1875], 2.
6 Bird, Isabella, vol. 1, 32.
7 Flaubert, vol. 2, 342; Belgiojoso 1855: 2, 1026.
8 Tinne quoted in Gladstone, 215; Duff Gordon 1983 [1902], 38.
9 Gasparin, 53–54.
10 Fagnani, 150–51.
11 Burton 1879 [1875], 88.
12 Audouard, 30.
13 Nisbet, 51.
14 Audouard, 38.
15 Montagu, vol. 1, 348–49.
16 [Meryon], *Travels,* vol. 2, 259; Bell 1927, 216; Belgiojoso 1855: 1, 472; Jebb, 301.
17 Loti, 101–102.
18 Duff Gordon 1983 [1902], 297.
19 Marianne-Elisa de Lamartine quoted in Lamartine, vol. 2, 115.

20 Duff Gordon 1983 [1902], 143–44.
21 Ibid., 41.
22 Burton 1879 [1875], 159; 1893, 571.
23 Edwards, 163–64.
24 Jebb, 286, 287, 292.
25 Forbes 1928, 56.
26 [Meryon], *Travels,* vol. 2, 25–26n.
27 Engel, 58.
28 Clarke, 320.
29 Nerval, 208.
30 Flaubert, vol. 1, 149.
31 Sattin, 84–85; Flaubert, vol. 1, 102.
32 Nightingale, 197.
33 Duff Gordon 1983 [1902], 96.
34 Fountaine, 167.
35 Duff Gordon 1983 [1902], 108.
36 Ibid., 161.
37 Lovell, xv: Mary Lovell's research involved deciphering Digby's coded diaries; Fountaine, 13; Kobak, 239–41.
38 Burton and Wilkins, 395.
39 Beaufort, vol. 1, 330.
40 Fountaine, 134.
41 Fountaine, 130, 132, 137–38, 162–63.
42 Kobak, 132, 134–35, 149.
43 Butcher, Charles, 9.
44 Butcher, E. L., 171.
45 Lovell, 271, 276; Fountaine, 156.
46 Porter, vol. 2, 507.
47 Bernoville, 30, 31.
48 Burton 1879 [1875], 278–79.
49 Sykes, 168.
50 Bell 1907, 268.
51 Report to the Judicial Department, Government of Bombay, 7 January 1913, quoted in Levine, 255.
52 Hyam, 147.
53 Bird, Michael, 85, 101, 104.
54 Ibid., 123.
55 Nisbet, 114.
56 Carré, vol. 1, 268.
57 Kobak, 230; Maillart, 94.
58 Burton 1893, 575; 1879 [1875], 93.
59 Duff Gordon, 1983 [1902], 142.
60 Ibid., 182.
61 Edwards, 454.

THE JOURNEY'S END: pages 171–73
Epigraph: Jebb, 301.
1 Ibid., 15.
2 *Illustrated London News,* 13 November 1858, 444; *Blackwood's,* July 1896, 49.

# BIBLIOGRAPHY

Addison, Charles G. *Damascus and Palmyra: A Journey to the East*, vol. 1. London: Richard Bentley, 1838.

Allemagne, Henry-René d'. *Les Saint-Simoniens: 1827–1837*. Paris: Librairie Gründ, 1930.

————. *Prosper Enfantin et les grandes entreprises du XIXe siècle*. Paris: Librairie Gründ, 1935.

Arnaud-Duc, Nicole. "The Law's Contradictions," in *A History of Women in the West: IV. Emerging Feminism from Revolution to World War*. Translated by Arthur Goldhammer. Edited by Geneviève Fraisse and Michelle Perrot. Cambridge: The Belknap Press of Harvard University Press, 1993.

Asher, Michael. *Thesiger*. New York: Viking, 1994.

Audouard, Olympe (de Jouval). *Les Mystères de l'Égypte dévoilés*. 2nd ed. Paris: E. Dentu, 1866.

Augri, Muriel, and Enrichetta Leospo. *Viaggio in Egitto: Racconti di donne dell'Ottocento*. Turin: Centre Culturel Français de Turin, 1998.

Barbiera, Raffaello. *Passioni del risorgimento: nuove pagine sulla Principessa Belgiojoso e il suo tempo con documenti inediti e illustrazioni*. Milano: Treves, 1903.

Beaufort, Emily A. *Egyptian Sepulchres and Syrian Shrines*. 2 vols. London: Longman, Green, Longman, & Roberts, 1861.

Belgiojoso, Cristina di. "La Vie intime et la vie nomade en Orient, scènes et souvenirs de voyage," in *Revue des deux mondes*. 1: 1 février 1855, tome 9, 466–501; 2: 1 mars 1855, tome 9, 1020–50; 3: 1 avril 1855, tome 10, 60–90; 4: 1 septembre 1855, tome 11, 1201–33.

————. *Asie Mineure et Syrie, souvenirs de voyages*. Paris: M. Lévy, 1858.

Bell, Gertrude. *The Desert and the Sown*. London: Heinemann, 1907.

————. *The Letters of Gertrude Bell*, vol. 1. Lady Florence Bell, editor. London: Ernest Benn, 1927.

————. Unpublished letter to Hugh Bell, 27 December 1918; to Frank Balfour, 17 December 1921. Gertrude Bell Archives, University of Newcastle, UK.

Belzoni, Mrs [Sarah]. *A Short Account of the Women of Egypt, Nubia, and Syria*, in

*Narrative of the Operations and Recent Discoveries in Egypt and Nubia*. London: John Murray, 1820.

Bernoville, Raphaël. *Dix Jours en Palmyrène*. Paris: Typographie A. Lainé & J. Havard, 1868.

Bird, Isabella Lucy. *Journeys in Persia and Kurdistan: Including a Summer in the Upper Karun Region and a Visit to the Nestorian Rayahs*. 2 vols. London: John Murray, 1891.

Bird, Michael. *Samuel Shepheard of Cairo*. London: Michael Joseph, 1957.

*Blackwood's*. Review, "Mrs Poole's 'Englishwoman in Egypt,'" March 1845, 286–97.

————. Review, "Lady Travellers," July 1896, 49–66.

Blunt, Lady Anne. *Bedouin Tribes of the Euphrates*. 2 vols. London: John Murray, 1879.

————. *Journals and Correspondence, 1878–1917*. Edited by Rosemary Archer and James Fielding. Cheltenham, UK: Alexander Heriot, 1986.

————. "Pèlerinage au Nedjed, berceau de la race arabe," in *Tour du Monde* 43: 1882, 1–80.

————. *A Pilgrimage to Nejd: The Cradle of the Arab Race. A Visit to the Court of the Arab Emir, and "Our Persian Campaign."* 2 vols. London: John Murray, 1881.

Brassey, Lady Annie. *Sunshine and Storm in the East*. 2 parts. London: Longmans, Green, 1880.

————. *The Last Voyage, 1886–1887*. London: Longmans, Green, 1889.

Bruce, Ian, editor. *The Nun of Lebanon: The Love Affair of Lady Hester Stanhope and Michael Bruce*. London: Collins, 1951.

Burgoyne, Elizabeth, editor. *Gertrude Bell: From Her Personal Papers, 1914–1926*. 2 vols. London: Ernest Benn, 1958 and 1961.

Burton, Lady Isabel. *The Inner Life of Syria, Palestine, and the Holy Land*. London: C. Kegan Paul, 1879 (first published 1875).

————. *The Life of Sir Richard F. Burton*, vol. 1. London: Chapman & Hall, 1893.

Burton, Lady Isabel, and W. H. Wilkins. *The Romance of Isabel Lady Burton: The Story of Her Life*. London: Hutchinson, 1898.

Butcher, Charles Henry. "Englishwomen in Egypt," letter to the *Times* (London), 3 January 1899, 9.

Butcher, E. L. *Egypt as We Knew It.* London: Mills & Boon, [1911].

Butler, Lady Elizabeth. *From Sketch-book and Diary.* London: Adam & Charles Black, 1909.

Carré, Jean-Marie. *Voyageurs et écrivains français en Égypte.* 2 vols. Cairo: L'Institut Français d'Archéologie Orientale, 1956 (first published 1932).

Clarke, E. D. *Travels in Various Countries of Europe, Asia and Africa,* vol. 5. London: T. Cadell & W. Davies, 1817.

Cleveland, Duchess of. *The Life and Letters of Lady Hester Stanhope.* London: John Murray, 1914.

Colet, Louise. *Lui: A View of Him.* Translated by Marilyn Gaddis Rose. Athens, GA: University of Georgia Press, 1986 (first published in French, 1859).

———. *Les Pays lumineux, voyage en Orient.* Paris: Dentu, 1879.

Craven, Lady Elizabeth. *A Journey Through the Crimea to Constantinople in a series of Letters from the Right Honourable Elizabeth Lady Craven, to His Serene Highness The Margrave of Brandenbourg, Anspach, and Bareith.* Dublin: Printed for H. Chamberlaine, R. Moncrieffe, W. Colles, G. Burnet, W. Wilson, L. White, P. Byrne, P. Wogan, H. Colbert, J. Moore, J. Jones, and B. Dornin, 1789.

Cunnington, Cecil Willett. *English Women's Clothing in the Nineteenth Century.* New York: Dover, 1990 (first published 1937).

Dieulafoy, Jane. "La Perse, la Chaldée et la Susiane, 1881–1882," in *Tour du monde* 46: 1883, 81–166.

———. *La Perse, la Chaldée et la Susiane.* Paris: Hachette, 1887.

"Divorce," in *The Encyclopedia Britannica,* vol. 7. Philadelphia: J. M. Stoddart, 1878, 260–65.

Dodd, Anna Bowman. *In the Palaces of the Sultan.* New York: Dodd, Mead, 1903.

Dronsart, Marie. *Les Grandes voyageuses.* Paris: Hachette, 1894.

Dufferin, Lord, editor. *Lispings from Low Latitudes; or, Extracts from the Journal of the Honourable Impulsia Gushington.* London: John Murray, 1863.

Duff Gordon, Lady Lucie. *Letters from Egypt: 1862–1869.* Edited by Gordon Waterfield. London: Routledge & Kegan Paul, 1969 (first published 1865).

———. *Letters from Egypt: 1862–1869.* With a memoir by her daughter Janet Ross. London: Virago, 1983 (this edition first published 1902).

———. *Last Letters from Egypt, to which are added Letters from the Cape.* With a memoir by her daughter Janet Ross. London: Macmillan, 1875.

[Eastlake, Lady Elizabeth]. "Lady Travellers," in *Quarterly Review* 151: 1845, 98–137.

Eberhardt, Isabelle. "Reminiscences," in *Prisoner of Dunes: Selected Writings.* Translated by Sharon Bangert. London: Peter Owen, 1995.

Ebers, Georg Moritz. *L'Égypte, Alexandrie et Le Caire,* vol. 1; *Du Caire à Philæ,* vol. 2. Translated by Gaston Maspero. Paris: Firmin-Didot, 1883 (first published in German, 1879).

Edidin, Stephen R. "Les Orientalismes de Gérôme," in *Gérôme & Goupil, Art et Enterprise.* Paris: Éditions de la Réunion des musées nationaux, 2000.

Edwards, Amelia B. *A Thousand Miles Up the Nile.* London: George Routledge, 1888 (first published 1877).

Egerton, Lady Francis [Harriet Catherine, Countess of Ellesmere]. *Journal of a Tour in the Holy Land, in May and June, 1840.* London: Harrison, 1841.

Engel, Regula. *L'Amazone de Napoléon, Mémoires de Regula Engel.* Translated by Jean-Jacques Fiechter. Paris: Olivier Orban, 1985 (first published in German, 1821).

Fagnani, Mme. "A State Ball in Constantinople," in *Scribner's,* June 1877, 148–51.

Fay, Mrs Eliza. *Original Letters from India: Containing a Narrative of a Journey Through Egypt, and the Author's Imprisonment at Calicut by Hyder Ally: 1779–1815.* Introduction by E. M. Forster. London: Hogarth Press, 1925 (first published Calcutta, 1817).

Finch, Edith. *Wilfrid Scawen Blunt, 1840–1922.* London: Jonathan Cape, 1938.

Flaubert, Gustave. *Notes de voyages,* vol. 1: *Italie, Égypte, Palestine, Rhodes;* vol. 2: *Asie Mineure, Constantinople, Grèce, Italie, Carthage.* Paris: Louis Conard, 1910.

Forbes, Rosita. *Adventure.* Boston: Houghton Mifflin, 1928.

———. *The Secret of the Sahara: Kufara.* London: Cassell, 1921.

Fountaine, Margaret. *Love Among the Butterflies: The Secret Life of a Victorian Lady.* Edited by W. F. Cater. Boston: Little, Brown, 1980.

Gasparin, Valérie Boissier de. *Journal d'un voyage au Levant,* vol 2. Paris: Michel Lèvy, 1866.

Gauthier, Maximilien. *Achille et Eugène Devéria.* Paris: H. Floury, 1925.

Gladstone, Penelope. *Travels of Alexine: Alexine Tinne, 1835–1869.* London: John Murray, 1970.

Gordon, Felicia, and Máire Cross. *Early French Feminisms, 1830–1940: A Passion for Liberty.* Cheltenham, UK: Edward Elgar, 1996.

Gray, Francine du Plessix. *Rage and Fire: A Life of Louise Colet, Pioneer Feminist, Literary Star, Flaubert's Muse*. New York: Simon & Schuster, 1994.

Haja, Martina, and Günther Wimmer. *Les Orientalistes des écoles Allemande et Autrichienne*. Translated into French by Manuel Chemineau. Paris: ACR Édition, 2000.

Hamel, Frank. *Lady Hester Lucy Stanhope*. London: Cassell, 1913.

Hanson, Captain. *Route of Lieutenant-General Sir Miles Nightingall, K.C.B. Overland from India, in a Series of Letters*. London: T. Baker, 1820.

Hassanein, Ahmed Mohammed. *The Lost Oases*. London: Thornton Butterworth, 1925.

Hornby, Lady [Emilia Bithynia, Mrs Edmund]. *Constantinople During the Crimean War*. London: Richard Bentley, 1863 (first published as *In and Around Stamboul*, 1858).

Hyam, Ronald. *Empire and Sexuality: The British Experience*. Manchester: Manchester University Press, 1992.

*Illustrated London News*. Review, "Madame Ida Pfeiffer," 13 November 1858, 444.

Ivray, Jehan d'. *L'Aventure Saint-Simonienne et les femmes*. Paris: Félix Alcan, 1928.

Izzard, Molly. *Freya Stark: A Biography*. London: Hodder & Stoughton, 1993.

Jebb, Louisa. *By Desert Ways to Baghdad*. Edinburgh: Thomas Nelson & Sons, 1908.

Jérusalémy, M.F. "Moeurs Turques: Les femmes turques, leur vie et leurs plaisirs," in *Tour du monde* 8: 1863, 145–54.

Joanne, Adolphe, and Émile Isambert. *Itinéraire descriptif, historique et archéologique de l'Orient*. Paris: Hachette, 1861.

Kobak, Annette. *Isabelle: The Life of Isabelle Eberhardt*. New York: Vintage, 1990.

Lamartine, Alphonse de. *Souvenirs, impressions, pensées et paysages pendant un voyage en orient, 1832–1833*. 2 vols. Paris: Charles Gosselin, 1849 (first published 1835).

Lane, Edward W., translator. *The Thousand and One Nights*. 2 vols. London: Chatto & Windus, 1883 (first published 1838–41).

Levine, Philippa. *Prostitution, Race, and Politics: Policing Venereal Disease in the British Empire*. New York: Routledge, 2003.

Lortet, M. "La Syrie d'aujourd'hui," in *Tour du monde* 39: 1880, 145–92.

Loti, Pierre [pseud. Julien Viaud]. *Egypt*. Translated by W.P. Baines. London: T. Werner Laurie, 1909.

Lott, Emmeline. *The "English governess" in Egypt. Harem life in Egypt and Constantinople*. Philadelphia: T.B. Peterson & Brothers, [1866].

Lovell, Mary S. *Rebel Heart: The Scandalous Life of Jane Digby*. New York: W.W. Norton, 1995.

Maillart, Ella. *Turkestan Solo*. London: Century, 1985 (first published 1934).

Manley, Deborah. "Lord Belmore Proceeds up the Nile in 1817–1818," in *Unfolding the Orient*. Edited by Paul and Janet Starkey. Reading, UK: Ithaca Press, 2001.

Martineau, Harriet. *Eastern Life, Present and Past*. Philadelphia: Lea & Blanchard, 1848.

[Meryon, Charles Lewis]. *Memoirs of the Lady Hester Stanhope: As Related by Herself in Conversations With Her Physician; Comprising Her Opinions and Anecdotes of Some of the Most Remarkable Persons of Her Time*, vols. 1 and 3. London: H. Colburn, 1846.

———. *Travels of Lady Hester Stanhope: Forming the Completion of Her Memoirs. Narrated by Her Physician*. 3 vols. London: H. Colburn, 1846.

Micklewright, Nancy. *A Victorian Traveler in the Middle East: The Photography and Travel Writing of Annie Lady Brassey*. Aldershot, UK: Ashgate, 2003.

Montagu, Lady Mary Wortley. *The Letters and Works of Lady Mary Wortley Montagu*, vols. 1 and 2. Edited by Lord Wharncliffe. London: Richard Bentley, 1837.

Montagu, Lady Mary Wortley. *Letters of the Right Honourable Lady M--y W---y M---e*. Berlin, 1781.

Montesquieu, Charles-Louis, Baron de. *Persian and Chinese Letters, being the Lettres Persanes*. Translated by John Davidson. Washington, DC: M. Walter Dunne, 1901.

Moon, Brenda E. "Amelia Edwards, Jennie Land and Egypt," in *Interpreting the Orient: Travellers in Egypt and the Near East*. Edited by Paul and Janet Starkey. Reading, UK: Ithaca Press, 2001.

Moore, Thomas. "Lalla Rookh: an Oriental Romance," in *Moore's Poetical Works*. London: London Printing & Publishing, c. 1880 (first published 1817).

Nerval, Gerard de. *Voyage en Orient*, vol 1. Paris: François Bernouard, 1927 (first published between 1840 and 1851).

Nightingale, Florence. *Letters from Egypt: A Journey on the Nile, 1849–1850*. Edited by Anthony Sattin. New York: Weidenfeld & Nicolson, 1987.

Nisbet, Mary. *The Letters of Mary Nisbet of Dirleton, Countess of Elgin*. Edited by Lieutenant-Colonel Nisbet Hamilton Grant. London: John Murray, 1926.

O'Neill, Patricia. "Amelia Edwards: From Novelist to Egyptologist," in *Interpreting the Orient: Travellers in Egypt and the Near East*. Edited by Paul and Janet Starkey. Reading, UK: Ithaca Press, 2001.

Pardoe, Miss Julia. *The Beauties of the Bosphorus
. . . Illustrated in a Series of Views of
Constantinople and Its Environs, From
Original Drawings by W. H. Bartlett,* vols. 1
and 4. London: Virtue & Co., 1839.

Paston, George. *Little Memoirs of the Eighteenth
Century.* New York: E.P. Dutton, 1901.

Perrot, Michelle. "Stepping Out," in *A History
of Women in the West: IV. Emerging Feminism
from Revolution to World War.* Translated by
Arthur Goldhammer. Edited by Geneviève
Fraisse and Michelle Perrot. Cambridge:
The Belknap Press of Harvard University
Press, 1993.

Pfeiffer, Ida. *The Last Travels of Ida Pfeiffer;
inclusive of a visit to Madagascar.* London:
Routledge, Warne, & Routledge, 1861.

———. *A Visit to the Holy Land, Egypt, and
Italy.* London: Ingram, Cooke, 1852.

———. *A Woman's Journey Around the World,
from Vienna to Brazil, Chili, Tahiti, China,
Hindostan, Persia, and Asia Minor.* London:
Office of the National Illustrated Library,
c. 1851.

Porter, J. L. *Murray's Hand-Book to Syria and
Palestine.* 2 vols. London: John Murray,
1868 [1871].

Rodenbeck, John. "Dressing Native," in
*Unfolding the Orient: Travellers in Egypt
and the Near East.* Edited by Paul and
Janet Starkey. Reading, UK: Ithaca Press,
2001.

Ross, Alexander M. *William Henry Bartlett:
Artist, Author, and Traveller.* Toronto:
University of Toronto Press, 1973.

Sackville-West, Vita. *Passenger to Teheran.*
London: Cockbird Press, 1990 (first
published 1926).

Sattin, Anthony. *Lifting the Veil: British Society
in Egypt 1768–1956.* London: J. M. Dent,
1988.

Searight, Sarah. *The British in the Middle East.*
New York: Atheneum, 1970.

Seton, Grace Thompson. *A Woman Tenderfoot
In Egypt.* New York: Dodd, Mead, 1923.

Stark, Freya. *Beyond Euphrates: Autobiography
1928–33.* London: John Murray, 1951.

———. *The Coast of Incense: Autobiography
1933–39.* London: John Murray, 1953.

Stebbing, Henry. *The Christian in Palestine.*
With drawings by W. H. Bartlett. London:
George Virtue, [1847].

Steegmuller, Francis, editor and translator.
*Flaubert in Egypt: A Sensibility on Tour.*
Chicago: Academy Chicago, 1979 (first
published 1972).

Stéphan, Raoul. *Isabelle Eberhardt ou la
révélation du Sahara.* Paris: Flammarion, 1930.

Stoddart, Anna. *The Life of Isabella Bird (Mrs.
Bishop).* London: John Murray, 1906.

Sykes, Ella C. *Through Persia on a Side-Saddle.*
London: A. D. Innes, 1901.

Thomson, W. M. *The Land and the Book; or,
Biblical Illustrations Drawn from the Manners
and Customs, the Scenes and Scenery of The
Holy Land.* London: T. Nelson, 1880.

*Times* (London). Review, "Countess Ida von
Hahn-Hahn's *Letters from the Orient,*"
17 September 1845, 8.

Trollope, Anthony. "An Unprotected Female
at the Pyramids," in *Anthony Trollope:
Tourists and Colonials,* vol. 3. Fort Worth:
Texas Christian University Press, 1981 (first
published 1860).

———. "The Unprotected Female Tourist,"
in *Travelling Sketches.* New York: Arno,
1981 (first published 1865).

Waller, John Francis, editor. *The Imperial
Dictionary of Universal Biography,* vol. 12.
London: William Mackenzie, c. 1880.

Wilkie, Sir David. *Sir David Wilkie Sketches:
Turkey, Syria and Egypt, 1840 and 1841.*
Drawn on stone by Joseph Nash. London:
Graves & Warmsley, 1843.

Wilkinson, Sir J. Gardner. *Murray's Hand-Book
for Travellers to Egypt.* London: John
Murray, 1858 [1862].

Wilson, Colonel. *Picturesque Palestine.* 2 vols.
New York: Appleton, 1881.

Winstone, H. V. F. *Gertrude Bell.* Rev. ed.
London: Constable, 1993 (first published
1978).

"Women," in *The Encyclopedia Britannica,*
vol. 24. Philadelphia: J. M. Stoddart, 1889,
671–77.

Yeazell, Ruth Bernard. *Harems of the Mind:
Passages of Western Art and Literature.* New
Haven: Yale University Press, 2000.

Zurcher, Monsieur, and Monsieur Margollé.
"Mademoiselle Tinne ," in *Tour du monde*
21: 1870–71, 289–304.

# ACKNOWLEDGMENTS

I would like to thank everyone who suggested women travelers; I wish I could have included them all. I'm grateful to the following for their help with my research: Laurence Budik, for image material; Mary Lovell, for information on Jane Digby's portrait; Joyce Williams and Don Clark of Joyce Williams Prints and Maps, for the loan in the Sir David Wilkie lithographs; Derryl MacLean, associate professor of the Department of History at Simon Fraser University, for his helpful source suggestions and for his expertise on linguistic details; Bettina Eschenhagen of Gerstenberg Verlag, for her information on German travelers to the East and especially for her information on Isabelle Eberhardt; Virginia Murray of John Murray Archives, for graciously permitting me to reprint the photograph of Freya Stark; Jim Crow of the Gertrude Bell Archives at the University of Newcastle, for arranging the loan of the Gertrude Bell images; James Kilvington, of the National Portrait Gallery, for his help regarding Lady Mary Wortley Montagu's portrait; Victoria Steele, Deborah Whiteman, and Octavio Olvera of the Special Collections Department of the Charles E. Young Research Library, UCLA, for their assistance in the loan of the engraving of Lady Mary Wortley Montagu's visit to Turkish baths.

Thanks to my editor, Nancy Flight, for keeping me on track and to copyeditor Wendy Fitzgibbons, for her thoroughness and valuable comments.

My special thanks, as always, to David Gay.

## CHAPTER OPENING IMAGE CREDITS

Page 1: American women at a Turkish café, as envisioned by *Leslie's Ladies Magazine*, 1878; page 7: "Camel at Assûan," sketch by Amelia Edwards, from *A Thousand Miles Up the Nile*, 1888 [1877], 193; page 33: "On the Nile," sketch by Elizabeth Butler, *From Sketch-book and Diary*, 1909, 30; page 65: Roxane, from "Bajazet," *Œuvres de Racine*, 1852, act 3, scene 1; page 87: "Lady Dunya writes a letter," Edward W. Lane, *The Thousand and One Nights*, vol. 1, 1883, 523; page 109: the "Window of a Harem," Bernhard Fiedler, artist, Ebers, *L'Égypte*, vol. 1, 1883, 77; page 137: "The Khedive's [viceroy's] troops," sketch by Elizabeth Butler, *From Sketch-book and Diary*, 1909, 30; page 171: "Women of the Harem," Edward W. Lane, *The Thousand and One Nights*, vol. 2, 1883, 492.

# INDEX

Illustrations are indicated in *italics*. For book titles, please refer to the bibliography.